MENTAL RETARDATION

Definition, Classification, and Systems of Supports

9th Edition

American Association on Mental Retardation

Published by
American Association on Mental Retardation
1719 Kalorama Road, NW
Washington, DC 20009-2683

Library of Congress Cataloging-in-Publication Data
Mental retardation: definition, classification, and systems of supports.—9th edition.
    p. cm.
  Rev. ed. of: Classification in mental retardation. c1983.
  Includes bibliographical references and index.
  ISBN 0-940898-30-6: $65.00
1. Mental retardation—Classification. I. American Association on Mental Retardation.
II. Classification in mental retardation.
  [DNLM: 1. Mental Retardation—classification. WM 15 M549]
RC570.C515   1992
616.85'88'0012—dc20
DNLM/DLC
for Library of Congress   92-35787
                                             CIP

Printed in the United States of America

THE AD HOC COMMITTEE ON TERMINOLOGY AND CLASSIFICATION

Ruth Luckasson, JD, Chair
Professor of Special Education
Attorney at Law
Department of Special Education
University of New Mexico
Albuquerque, New Mexico

David L. Coulter, MD
Associate Professor of Pediatrics
    and Neurology
Director of Pediatric Neurology
Boston University School of Medicine
Boston City Hospital
Boston, Massachusetts

Edward A. Polloway, EdD
Professor of Special Education
School of Education and Human
    Development
Lynchburg College
Lynchburg, Virginia

Steven Reiss, PhD
Director, The Nisonger Center
The Ohio State University
Columbus, Ohio

Robert L. Schalock, PhD
Program Consultant
Mid Nebraska Mental Individual Services
Chairman, Department of Psychology
Hastings College
Hastings, Nebraska

Martha E. Snell, PhD
Professor
Curry School of Education
Department of Curriculum, Instruction
    and Special Education
University of Virginia
Charlottesville, Virginia

Deborah M. Spitalnik, PhD
Executive Director
University Affiliated Program of New Jersey
Associate Professor Clinical Pediatrics
University of Medicine & Dentistry of New Jersey
Robert Wood Johnson Medical School
Piscataway, New Jersey

Jack A. Stark, PhD
Department of Psychiatry
Creighton Nebraska Combined Program
Omaha, Nebraska

TABLE OF CONTENTS

Errata

Please excuse our error! Page 33 should be numbered page 31.
(Page 31 becomes 32, and page 32 becomes 33.)

Please make this correction in your book now to avoid confusion as
you read. Thank you.

Mental Retardation: Definition, Classification, and Systems of Supports, 9th
Edition
AAMR

ACKNOWLEDGEMENTS

Many individuals, through their support and assistance, contributed to the development of this definition and manual. The Association and the authors specifically thank Past Presidents Robert Griffith, James Ellis, Robert Bruininks, and Jack Stark and President Michael Dillon and the members of the Boards of Directors (1988–1992) for their unfailing commitment, support, encouragement, and direction during the process. We also acknowledge the ground-breaking efforts of previous AAMR Terminology and Classification Committees, whose work was an integral part of these continuing efforts.

We also thank the following individuals who made important contributions to the 9th edition: Elizabeth Boggs, David Braddock, M. Doreen Croser, Paula Hirt, Denis Keyes, Paula Lucero, Frank Menolascino, Viki Morrison, Dan Reschly, Peggy Seiter, and Mahalah Stromquist. For her gracious and generous contributions in editing and production, we thank Yvette Taylor. Colleagues at each of the authors' universities provided considerable support: the University of New Mexico Department of Special Education, Boston University Medical School, Lynchburg College Department of Education, University of Illinois at Chicago Developmental Disabilities Center, Hastings College Department of Psychology, University of Medicine and Dentistry of New Jersey Robert Wood Johnson Medical School University Affiliated Program, University of Virginia Special Education Department, and Creighton-Nebraska University Medical School Department of Psychiatry.

Thoughtful reactions were received from concerned individuals, AAMR divisions, and sister organizations at critical stages of the development of the definition and the manual. The following individuals provided written comments at various stages of the work. The work benefitted from their input, but we were unable to incorporate every contribution. Ultimate content and editorial decisions were made by the Committee, and listing of an individual indicates assistance, not necessarily agreement.

The Association and the authors express gratitude to all those, named and unnamed, who so generously contributed their time and expertise to this effort.

John W. Ashbaugh
Donnell C. Ashford
James S. Baker
George S. Baroff
Michael J. Begab
Elizabeth Boggs
George N. Bouthilet
David Braddock
Robert H. Bradley
Robert Bruininks
Richard Burr
Mary C. Cerreto
Alan D. B. Clarke
Ann M. Clarke
Deborah E. Cohen
Paul D. Cotten

Liz Curren
Gloria Curry
Curt Decker
Michael R. Dillon
Sharon Borthwick Duffy
Barb Elliott
James W. Ellis
Richard K. Eyman
Nirhan Findykian
Donna Fletcher
Martha E. Ford
Steven R. Forness
William I. Gardner
Bill Gaventa
David A. Goode
Robert G. Griffith

Tamar Heller
Pierre S. Helmrath
Daniel Holdrinet
Ruth Humphry
Cherie Hymes
John W. Jacobson
Stephen E. Jones
Ruth Katz
Kim Keprios
Lars Kibbon
Charles Kimber
Marty Wyngaarden Krauss
Jay Kuder
Charlie Lakin
Lyle L. Lloyd
Maria del Carmen Malbran

ACKNOWLEDGEMENTS

Dianne Manfredini
Horace Mann
Paul Marchand
Edwin W. Martin
Johnny L. Matson
Gary Mattson
Paul R. Maurice
Sandra McClennen
Deborah L. McFadden
Ken McGill
Kathleen H. McGinley
Kevin McGrew
Chris Metzler

Diane Morin
Donald Morris
Hugo W. Moser
Michael Mulcahy
John Niederbuhl
Donald E. Noble
Trevor R. Parmenter
Roger K. Peters
Daniel J. Reschly
Marilyn Riddle
Robert Rueda
Martha C. Sabin
Donald F. Schneiderman

Marsha Mailick Seltzer
Wayne Silverman
Stu Smith
Judy Smith-Davis
Carrie Solmundson
Scott Spreat
Frederick A. Stiemke
Ludwik S. Szymanski
Lawrence T. Tafts
Marc Tasse
Sue Allen Warren
Richard Woodhouse
Ric Zaharia

PREFACE

Since its founding in 1876, the American Association on Mental Retardation (AAMR) has led the field of mental retardation in understanding, defining, and classifying the phenomenon of mental retardation. The Association has attempted to fulfill its responsibility by formulating and disseminating manuals and related information on terminology and classification through the years.

The AAMR's first edition of a manual on definition was published in 1921 in conjunction with the National Committee for Mental Hygiene. A second edition of that manual was published in 1933, and a third in 1941. The AAMR's (then the American Association on Mental Deficiency, AAMD) Committee on Nomenclature published the fourth edition in 1957, an etiological classification system.

The fifth edition, a comprehensive manual on terminology and classification, was published in 1959 (Heber, 1959) and reprinted with minor corrections in 1961 (Heber, 1961). Two dramatic changes in the 1959 manual included raising the IQ ceiling to one standard deviation below the mean (that is, an IQ of approximately 85 or below) and the formal introduction of an adaptive behavior criterion to the Association's definition of mental retardation.

The sixth edition (Grossman, 1973) lowered the IQ ceiling to two standard deviations below the mean (that is, an IQ of about 70 or below). Several other important changes introduced in the 1973 manual included inserting the word *significantly* before the term *subaverage general intellectual functioning*, raising the limit of the developmental period from age 16 to 18, and omitting the borderline level of retardation (that is, IQ about 70 to 85). The seventh edition (1977) included a series of relatively minor corrections and changes, and the eighth edition (Grossman, 1983) further clarified that the upper IQ range for the diagnosis was a guideline and with clinical judgment could extend to approximately 75.

This manual is the 9th edition of the regularly published definition and classification work of the Association. It is based on an evolving understanding of the concept of mental retardation and how it can be best defined and classified in our times. The present status of understanding mental retardation reflects years of work, research, contributions, and policy development by many persons in this field.

Although some aspects of the AAMR's 1983 definition and classification system remain the same (for example, the IQ guidelines of approximately 70 to 75 or below), this manual departs from previous editions in a number of ways. Four of the most important include:

1. It is an attempt to express the changing understanding of what mental retardation is;

2. It is a formulation of what ought to be classified as well as how to describe the systems of supports people with mental retardation require;

3. It represents a paradigm shift, from a view of mental retardation as an absolute trait expressed solely by an individual to an expression of the interaction between the person with limited intellectual functioning and the environment; and

4. It attempts to extend the concept of adaptive behavior another step, from a global description to specification of particular adaptive skill areas.

In 1988, AAMR President Robert Griffith appointed the present ad hoc Committee on Terminology and Classification. Thus began an open, dynamic, and, we believe, responsive process to express the contemporary understanding of mental retardation. At one level, the Committee reviewed the literature, research, and other writings on the meaning of mental retardation in the field of mental retardation and across disciplines. At another level, we surveyed current practice and understanding by direct workers in the field of mental retardation, families and friends of individuals, and individuals themselves who have the disability.

The process of attempting to form this information into a comprehensive definition and system of classification required many drafts. The input of a large number of people proved essential to the creative work: the general membership of the Association, members represented in leadership positions, members in divisions and special interest groups, individuals representing sister organizations and agencies, and other colleagues in the field. Activities included newsletter calls for comments, meetings at conventions, several Open Forums, targeted reviews, and the collection of targeted utilization data. In addition, an Advisory Group generously provided their input in the form of ideas, comments, and substantive help. The Association remains particularly suited to this work because of its interdisciplinary membership and its strong international ties.

After regular review by the Association's Board of Directors over the 4 years of development of the manual, The Board unanimously approved the definition at its 1992 Convention, "New Realities, New Challenges" in New Orleans.

We believe that you will find the changes in the manual helpful in understanding and working in the field of mental retardation. The changes reflect a changing paradigm, a more functional definition, and a focus on the interaction between the person, the environment, and the intensities and pattern of needed supports. The major changes are:

1. The global term *adaptive behavior* has been extended to 10 specific adaptive skill areas;

2. Four assumptions for the application of the definition are asserted at the same time as the definition; and

3. Rather than requiring subclassification into four levels of a person's mental retardation (mild, moderate, severe, and profound), the system subclassifies the intensities and pattern of supports systems into four levels (intermittent, limited, extensive, and pervasive).

This manual also emphasizes the importance of clinical judgment in the diagnosis and classification of mental retardation. All individuals are rich in complexities and uniqueness. Each person with mental retardation is a complex human being whose intellectual and adaptive limitations, psychological and emotional strengths and weaknesses, physical and health status, etiology of the condition, and environmental demands are his or hers alone. State-of-the-art clinical expertise and judgment is required to diagnose and classify the person's disability and systems of needed supports.

The manual retains the term *mental retardation*. Many individuals with this disability urge elimination of the term because it is stigmatizing and is frequently mistakenly used as a global summary about complex human beings. After considerable deliberation, we concluded that we were unable at this time to eliminate the term, despite its acknowledged shortcomings. The purpose of this manual was to define and create a contemporary system of classification for the disability currently known as mental retardation and, in order to accomplish that, we had to use the commonly understood term for the disability.

The next few years will be the transition period into the new definition and classification system. This will be a dynamic process. Predictably, transition in adoption and implementation of a new definition requires time. The changes in this definition and classification system are similar to changes in other arenas important to the lives of individuals with mental retardation and their families, such as eligibility standards in public benefits. Some areas in which transition to the new system is already occurring include conducting and publishing research, determining eligibility for services, funding public services, funding research and training, stimulating instrument development, conducting court-related and forensic work, and training professionals in the new definition.

The tradition of the American Association on Mental Retardation has been to lead the profession and society in promoting increased understanding of mental retardation and to support people with this disability to attain their goals through services they may need, protection of their rights as citizens, and supports to establish personal life satisfaction. This tradition is represented in the 1992 AAMR Definition, Classification, and Systems of Supports. The Association is grateful to be able to build on its more than 100 years of collegial work in our attempts to understand and assist individuals with mental retardation.

DEFINITION OF MENTAL RETARDATION

Mental retardation refers to substantial limitations in present functioning. It is characterized by significantly subaverage intellectual functioning, existing concurrently with related limitations in two or more of the following applicable adaptive skill areas: communication, self-care, home living, social skills, community use, self-direction, health and safety, functional academics, leisure, and work. Mental retardation manifests before age 18.

APPLICATION OF THE DEFINITION

The following four assumptions are essential to the application of the definition:

1. Valid assessment considers cultural and linguistic diversity as well as differences in communication and behavioral factors;

2. The existence of limitations in adaptive skills occurs within the context of community environments typical of the individual's age peers and is indexed to the person's individualized needs for supports;

3. Specific adaptive limitations often coexist with strengths in other adaptive skills or other personal capabilities; and

4. With appropriate supports over a sustained period, the life functioning of the person with mental retardation will generally improve.

PART I

THE DEFINITION
OF MENTAL RETARDATION

CHAPTER 1
MENTAL RETARDATION DEFINED AND EXPLAINED

MENTAL RETARDATION DEFINED

Mental retardation refers to substantial limitations in present functioning. It is characterized by significantly subaverage intellectual functioning, existing concurrently with related limitations in two or more of the following applicable adaptive skill areas: communication, self-care, home living, social skills, community use, self-direction, health and safety, functional academics, leisure, and work. Mental retardation manifests before age 18.

The following four assumptions are essential to the application of the definition:

1. Valid assessment considers cultural and linguistic diversity as well as differences in communication and behavioral factors;

2. The existence of limitations in adaptive skills occurs within the context of community environments typical of the individual's age peers and is indexed to the person's individualized needs for supports;

3. Specific adaptive limitations often coexist with strengths in other adaptive skills or other personal capabilities; and

4. With appropriate supports over a sustained period, the life functioning of the person with mental retardation will generally improve.

EXPLANATION OF THE DEFINITION

Mental retardation refers to substantial limitations in present functioning . . . Mental retardation is defined as a fundamental difficulty in learning and performing certain daily life skills. The personal capabilities in which there must be a substantial limitation are conceptual, practical, and social intelligence. These three areas are specifically affected in mental retardation whereas other personal capabilities (e.g., health and temperament) may not be.

It is characterized by significantly subaverage intellectual functioning . . . This is defined as an IQ standard score of approximately 70 to 75 or below, based on assessment that includes one or more individually administered general intelligence tests developed for the purpose of assessing intellectual functioning. These data should be reviewed by a multidisciplinary team and validated with additional test scores or evaluative information.

Existing concurrently . . . The intellectual limitations occur at the same time as the limitations in adaptive skills.

With related limitations . . . The limitations in adaptive skills are more closely related to the intellectual limitation than to some other circumstances such as cultural or linguistic diversity or sensory limitation.

In two or more of the following applicable adaptive skill areas . . . Evidence of adaptive skill limitations is necessary because intellectual functioning alone is insufficient for a diagnosis of mental retardation. The impact on functioning of these limitations must be sufficiently comprehensive to encompass at least two adaptive skill areas, thus showing a generalized limitation and reducing the probability of measurement error.

Communication, self-care, home living, social skills, community use, self-direction, health and safety, functional academics, leisure, and work . . . These skill areas are central to successful life functioning and are frequently related to the need for supports for persons with mental retardation. Because the relevant skills within each adaptive skill area may vary with chronological age, assessment of functioning must be referenced to the person's chronological age.

Mental retardation manifests before age 18 . . . The 18th birthday approximates the age when individuals in this society typically assume adult roles. In other societies, a different age criterion might be determined to be more appropriate.

The following four assumptions are essential to the application of this definition . . . These statements are essential to the meaning of the definition and cannot be conceptually separated from the definition. Applications of the definition should include these statements. Each statement has clear implications for subsequent assessment and intervention.

1. *Valid assessment considers cultural and linguistic diversity as well as differences in communication and behavioral factors* . . . Failure to consider factors such as the individual's culture, language, communication, and behaviors may cause an assessment to be invalid. Sound professional judgment and the use of a multidisciplinary team appropriate to the individual and his or her particular needs and circumstances should enhance the validity of assessments.

2. *The existence of limitations in adaptive skills occurs within the context of community environments typical of the individual's age peers and is indexed to the person's individualized needs for support* . . . Community environments typical of the individual's age peers refer to homes, neighborhoods, schools, businesses, and other environments in which persons of the individual's age ordinarily live, learn, work, and interact. The concept of age peers should also include consideration of individuals of the same cultural or linguistic background. The determination of the limitations in adaptive skills goes together with an analysis of supports that can include services that the individual needs and supports in the environments.

3. *Specific adaptive limitations often coexist with strengths in other adaptive skills or other personal capabilities* . . . Individuals frequently have strengths in personal capabilities independent of mental retardation. Examples include: (a) an individual may have strengths in physical or social capabilities that exist independently of the adaptive skill limitations related to mental retardation (e.g., good health);

(b) an individual may have a strength in a particular adaptive skill area (e.g., social skills) while having difficulty in another skill area (e.g., communication); and (c) an individual may possess certain strengths within a particular specific adaptive skill, while at the same time having limitations within the same area (e.g., functional math and functional reading, respectively). Some of a person's strengths may be relative rather than absolute; thus, the strengths may be best understood when compared to the limitations in other skill areas.

4. *With appropriate supports over a sustained period, the life functioning of the person with mental retardation will generally improve . . . Appropriate supports* refer to an array of services, individuals, and settings that match the person's needs. Although mental retardation may not be of lifelong duration, it is likely that supports will be needed over an extended period of time. Thus, for many individuals, the need for supports will be lifelong. For other individuals, however, the need for supports may be intermittent. Virtually all persons with mental retardation will improve in their functioning as a result of effective supports and services. This improvement will enable them to be more independent, productive, and integrated into their community. In addition, if individuals are not improving significantly, this relative lack of improvement should be the basis for determining whether the current supports are effective and whether changes are necessary. Finally, in rare circumstances, the major objective should be to maintain current level of functioning or to slow regression over time.

CHAPTER 2
THEORETICAL BASIS OF THE DEFINITION

Mental retardation is not something you have, like blue eyes or a bad heart. Nor is it something you are, like being short or thin. It is not a medical disorder, although it may be coded in a medical classification of diseases (e.g., ICD-9, World Health Organization, 1978). Nor is it a mental disorder, although it may be coded in a classification of psychiatric disorders (e.g., DSM-III-R, American Psychiatric Association, 1987). *Mental retardation* refers to a particular state of functioning that begins in childhood and in which limitations in intelligence coexist with related limitations in adaptive skills. In this sense, it is a more specific term than *developmental disability* because the level of functioning is necessarily related to an intellectual limitation. As a statement about functioning, it describes the "fit" between the capabilities of the individual and the structure and expectations of the individual's personal and social environment. The level of functioning in mental retardation may have a specific etiology, such as Down syndrome, but mental retardation is not synonymous with the etiology. Another way of saying this is that etiology is not destiny: an individual who has a condition commonly associated with mental retardation may not necessarily function in a way that meets the definition of mental retardation. The conceptual model for defining mental retardation is not a medical model (although a medical model may describe the etiology) nor is it a psychopathological model (although a psychopathological model may describe thinking or behavior that coexists in some individuals with mental retardation). With this revision of its manual, the American Association on Mental Retardation (AAMR) introduces a functional model as the conceptual basis for the current definition of mental retardation.

The 1959 AAMR definition of mental retardation formally included the importance of functioning (Heber, 1959). The requirement that "subaverage intellectual functioning must be reflected by impairment in one or more of the following aspects of adaptive behavior: maturation, learning and social adjustment" (p. 3) recognized that the existence of intellectual limitations alone was not sufficient for a diagnosis of mental retardation. These limitations must result in a functional impairment in adaptive behavior in order for mental retardation to exist. The current definition of mental retardation continues to recognize the congruence of intellectual and adaptive limitations and, thus, is consistent with previous definitions. Furthermore, the present emphasis on functioning represents the continued development and refinement of ideas that have been central to the AAMR definition since 1959. It differs from previous definitions by also recognizing the importance of the environment and its impact on functioning. Compared to the definitions in previous AAMR manuals, the present definition specifies adaptive skill areas (and delineates how these skills should be documented), emphasizes the relation among limitations in intellectual and adaptive skills, environmental influences on the impact of these limitations, and the intensities of supports needed to improve functioning in the community.

The present definition states that mental retardation refers to substantial limitations in present functioning. This is an important shift in thinking. Mental retardation is not a *trait*, although it is influenced by certain characteristics or capabilities of the individual as described later. Rather, mental retardation is a *state* in which functioning is impaired in certain specific ways. This distinction between *trait* and *state* is central to understanding how the present definition broadens the concept of mental retardation and how it shifts the emphasis from measurement of traits to understanding the individual's actual functioning in daily living. Understanding this distinction between trait and state is facilitated by examining the structure of this concept of mental retardation.

GENERAL STRUCTURE OF THE DEFINITION

Mental retardation refers to a particular state of impaired functioning within the community, first manifested in childhood, in which limitations in intelligence coexist with related limitations in adaptive skills. For any person with mental retardation, the description of this state of functioning requires knowledge of the individual's capabilities and an understanding of the structure and expectations of the individual's personal and social environment.

The key elements in the definition of mental retardation are *capabilities* (or competencies), *environments*, and *functioning*. This is shown diagrammatically in Figure 2.1.

FIGURE 2.1   General Structure of the Definition of Mental Retardation

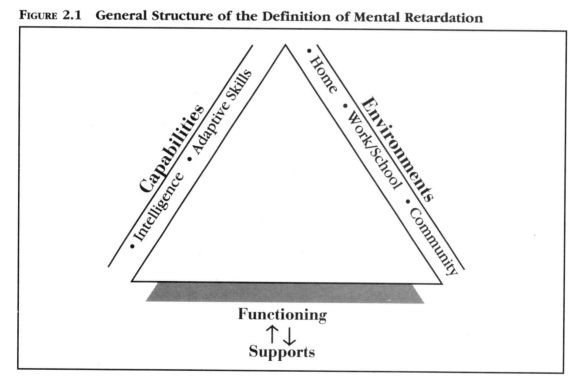

10

Figure 2.1 is structured with functioning as the base of the triangle to emphasize that this is primarily a functional model. Capabilities are shown on the left side of the triangle to indicate that functioning in mental retardation is specifically related to limitations in intelligence and in adaptive skills. This distinguishes the functional limitation in mental retardation from other states of limited functioning related to other causes, such as physical or emotional limitations. Placing these trait aspects on only one side of the triangle indicates that they are necessary but not sufficient for a full understanding of the concept of mental retardation. The right side of the triangle represents the environments in which individuals with mental retardation live, learn, play, work, socialize, and interact. The equilateral nature of the triangle indicates that a description of these environments is also necessary for a full understanding of the concept of mental retardation. By placing these components (capabilities and environments) on two sides of a single structure (the triangle), the model attempts to show that the interaction between them is central to the concept of mental retardation. The model also notes that the needs for support reflect how the individual functions and that the presence or absence of supports can reciprocally influence functioning. Supports are not included in the triangle, however, because they are not actually part of the concept of mental retardation but, rather, are responses to it.

Current thinking about the disabling process (Institute of Medicine, 1991) defines *functional limitation* as the effect of specific impairments on the performance or performance capability of the person. Thus, these limitations are described on the "capabilities" side of the triangle. *Disability* is the expression of such a limitation in a social context (Institute of Medicine, 1991). It reflects the interaction between limitations in intelligence and adaptive skills and the demands of the environment (home, work, school, and the community). Mental retardation is a disability *only* as a result of this interaction, according to this view of the disabling process. The model shown in Figure 2.1 depicts the disabling process for persons with mental retardation. It builds upon past theory and incorporates current thinking in a way that is intended to guide and shape future research and practice. Past and current thinking in each of these areas will be reviewed briefly to show how this model relates to current knowledge.

CAPABILITIES

The capabilities of the individual are described in the theory of general competence, which refers to those attributes that enable an individual to function in society (Greenspan, 1979, 1981, 1990). Certain attributes relate primarily to the individual's inner capabilities, and other attributes relate to the individual's ability to function in a social context. All people differ in their competencies in each of these areas, and many have strengths or weaknesses in one or more of these factors. The inner capability that is most relevant to the definition of mental retardation is conceptual intelligence, which encompasses cognition and learning. Other inner capabilities such as energy, stability of state, mobility, strength, sensation, and communication may be affected in some individuals with mental retardation, but they are not always affected and are not essential to the definition of mental retardation.

The aspects of social competence that are most relevant to the definition of mental retardation are the intellectual aspects, including both practical and social intelligence. Taken together, practical and social intelligence are the fundamental human capabilities that form the basis for adaptive skills. Other aspects of social competence such as personality, temperament, and character may be affected in some individuals with mental retardation, but they are not always affected and are not essential to the definition of mental retardation.

A similar model of personal competence has received some empirical support (McGrew and Bruininks, 1990). This model distinguishes five categories: physical competence, conceptual intelligence, practical intelligence, social competence, and emotional competence. The empirical studies supported the distinction of these categories as separate aspects of personal competence.

According to these concepts, mental retardation is a condition in which there are limitations in conceptual, practical, and social intelligence. This approach derives from Thorndike's (1920) original conceptualization of mental retardation as including limitations in abstract intelligence, mechanical (or practical) intelligence, and social intelligence. It also relates to Guilford's (1967) structure of intellect model, in which the content plane includes symbolic and semantic abilities (dimensions of abstract intelligence), figural abilities (a dimension of practical intelligence), and behavioral abilities (a dimension of social intelligence). Thus, the theoretical basis for the capability side of the current model of mental retardation (shown in Figure 2.1) is consistent with a long history of thinking and research. Furthermore, it emphasizes that mental retardation primarily refers to limitations in intelligence and reflects current thinking about different aspects or types of intelligence (see, for example, Gardner, 1983; Lohman, 1989).

For example, only certain types of intelligence are necessarily affected in mental retardation. Thus, individuals with mental retardation need not have limitations in other areas of personal competence and may indeed have strengths in some areas. Mental retardation refers to a specific pattern of intellectual limitation; it is not a state of global incompetence.

ENVIRONMENTS

Baumeister (1987) emphasized the need for a model of mental retardation that more closely balances individual capabilities and the demands and constraints of specific environments. This balance is depicted in Figure 2.1, in which environments and capabilities constitute equivalent sides of the current model. The environment is conceptualized as the specific settings in which the person lives, learns, plays, works, socializes, and interacts. Positive environments foster the growth, development, and well-being of the individual (Edgerton, 1988; Garber, 1988; Landesman and Vietze, 1987) and enhance the individual's quality of life (Schalock, 1990). For individuals with mental retardation, these positive environments constitute settings that are typical of their age peers and that are appropriate for the individuals' sociocultural background. It is within such settings that the individual with mental retardation is most likely to achieve optimal interdependence and productivity and to enjoy maximal inclusion in the life of the community.

Desirable environments for persons with mental retardation have three major characteristics: They provide opportunities for fulfilling the person's needs; they foster the person's well-being in physical, social, material, and cognitive life areas; and they promote the person's sense of stability, predictability, and control (Schalock and Kiernan, 1990). Less desirable environments are lacking in one or more of these characteristics. All persons with mental retardation live in an environment that may be analyzed in these terms and that can be measured as being more or less desirable for that individual. In chapter 8 we discuss how the environment can be described. The model of mental retardation incorporated in this manual (depicted in Figure 2.1) emphasizes that functioning can be influenced as much by the nature of the person's environment as it is by the person's capabilities. Furthermore, the types, roles, and intensities of supports needed to improve functioning can reflect these characteristics of the environment as much as they reflect the capabilities of the individual.

FUNCTIONING

Mental retardation is present when specific intellectual limitations affect the person's ability to cope with the ordinary challenges of everyday living in the community. If the intellectual limitations have no real effect on functioning, then the person does not have mental retardation. This implies a certain relativity of significance of the intellectual limitations, in which the significance of these limitations would be relative to the demands of the environment. Kanner (1949) pointed out that persons with intellectual limitations may be successful in less complex social situations that are less intellectually centered and may even be superior if they have other capabilities that are more prized or rewarded by the social context. He considered mental retardation as an ethnologically determined phenomenon relative to local standards and within those standards, to educational, vocational, and family expectancies.

The intellectual and adaptive skill limitations in mental retardation may affect functioning in a variety of ways. The relativity of significance means that there is no one way that defines "retarded" performance. Every person with mental retardation will differ in the nature, extent, and severity of their functional limitations, depending on the demands and constraints of their environment and the presence or absence of supports. The current definition reflects this fact by requiring the presence of limitations in two or more of a variety of adaptive skill areas but does not require any one single limitation or any specific combination of limitations.

A functional definition of developmental disabilities was incorporated in Public Law (PL) 95-682, the Developmental Disabilities Bill of Rights Act (1978). According to this definition, a *developmental disability* is attributable to a mental or physical impairment that begins before age 22 and is likely to continue indefinitely and that results in substantial functional limitation in *three* or more areas of major life activity. These areas are generally similar to the areas in which limitations in adaptive skills may occur according to the present definition of mental retardation. The requirement for substantial functional limitation in three or more major life areas was intended to assure provision of services to individuals with more severe impairments (Kiernan, Smith, and Ostrowsky, 1986). This requirement is most relevant to adolescents and adults because the life areas specified in the federal definition have little relevance for infants and limited relevance for young children. More recently, however, PL 99-457 (1989) specifically recognized the need for comprehensive early intervention services and enhanced educational services for infants and young children with disabilities, including those with mental retardation. In order to assure that infants, young children, and persons with less severe functional limitations receive all indicated services and supports, the present AAMR definition of mental retardation requires the existence of limitations in *two* or more adaptive skill areas. In this respect, the concept of functioning included in this definition of mental retardation is broader than that which is included in the current federal definition of developmental disabilities. On the other hand, the requirement for limitations in two or more adaptive skill areas reduces the possibility of over-inclusion, which might result if limitation in only one adaptive skill area were required because limitation related to possible errors in measurement of only one adaptive skill area will not suffice to determine the diagnosis of mental retardation. Furthermore, limitations in two or more adaptive skill areas will more likely reflect a general influence on life functioning.

THE INTELLECTUAL LIMITATION

The intellectual limitation in mental retardation is unfortunately often thought of only as a low IQ score on a standard intelligence test. In fact, the limitations of intelligence tests are well known and are discussed in chapter 4. It is important here to note that IQ is a score on a test and not necessarily the same as the fundamental intellectual capabilities affected in mental retardation. These capabilities are commonly thought to be measured by the intelligence test, but we note that the IQ is merely a convenient measure of this construct. The validity of the intelligence test—the extent to which it measures the individual's true intellectual capabilities—must be reasonably certain in order for it to be used for diagnostic purposes. When clinicians are faced with situations in which the validity of the IQ may be uncertain, such as the assessment of individuals with markedly different cultural, social, linguistic, family, and educational backgrounds, other sources of information about intellectual capabilities should be identified. When the existence of intellectual limitations is uncertain or equivocal, the decision should be made that would result in services that would be most advantageous to the individual. In other words, these equivocal situations reflect the relative significance of the measured IQ score in relation to the need for services.

Mental retardation is characterized by significantly subaverage intellectual capabilities or "low intelligence." If the IQ score is valid, this will generally result in a score of approximately 70 to 75 or below. This upper boundary of IQs for use in classification of mental retardation is flexible to reflect the statistical variance inherent in all intelligence tests and the need for clinical judgment by a qualified psychological examiner. If a valid IQ score is not possible, significantly subaverage intellectual capabilities means a level of performance that is less than that observed in the vast majority (approximately 97 percent) of persons of comparable background. In order to be valid, the assessment of intellectual performance must be free from errors caused by motor, sensory, emotional, language, or cultural factors.

The existence of intellectual limitations of this magnitude is a necessary but not sufficient condition for the definition of mental retardation. As noted previously, the intellectual limitations must have an impact on coping or adaptive skills to meet the definition. Practically speaking, one may argue that intellectual limitations of this magnitude will necessarily result in difficulties in adaptive skills, so that one need only document the intellectual limitations to establish the diagnosis of mental retardation. Such an argument does not deny the importance of adaptive limitations but argues that they are too difficult to measure to include as an essential component of the definition (Zigler and Hodapp, 1986). However, two predominant reasons can be cited for the importance of limitations in adaptive skills as an accompaniment to the cognitive limitations. First, consideration of adaptive skills provides confirmation of the existence of functional limitations when the validity of the IQ score is in question or when a borderline or equivocal condition prevails. Second, and more important, emphasizing the impact on adaptive skills reflects the linkage of these functional limitations to the need for services. By emphasizing the impact on functioning, the current definition intends to stimulate more research on valid measurement of adaptive skills, on the linkage of adaptive limitations with the need for services, and on the relation between services provided and benefits obtained.

THE ADAPTIVE LIMITATION

The adaptive difficulties in mental retardation derive from limitations in practical and social intelligence. *Practical intelligence* refers to the ability to maintain and sustain oneself as an independent person in managing the ordinary activities of daily living. It includes the capacity to use one's physical abilities (whatever they may be) to achieve the greatest degree of personal independence possible. Practical intelligence is central to such adaptive abilities as sensorimotor skills, self-care (sleeping, bathing, toileting, eating, and drinking) and safety skills (avoiding danger and preventing injury). It is also important for other adaptive abilities such as functional academics, work, leisure, self-direction, and use of the community.

Social intelligence refers to the ability to understand social expectations and the behavior of other persons and to judge appropriately how to conduct oneself in social situations. The principal components of social intelligence are social awareness and social skill. More specifically, they include social comprehension, insight, judgment, and communication. Individuals with mental retardation may have significant limitations in the ability to comprehend social behavior, including difficulty inferring personal cues through role-taking and difficulty inferring situational cues in interpersonal transactions. They may have significant limitations in their ability to exhibit social insight into the motivation and personal characteristics of others. They may have significant limitations in the ability to show good ethical judgment in their interpersonal behaviors and in the ability to communicate their own thoughts and feelings in solving problems when conflicting needs exist in social situations (Greenspan, 1979, 1981). Social intelligence is central to such adaptive abilities as social skills, communication, work, leisure, home living, and use of the community.

Practical and social intelligence act in concert to sustain the development of adaptive skills. The components of practical and social intelligence are not isomorphic or synonymous with the specific adaptive skills listed in the definition, however. As noted previously, at least some adaptive skills reflect both practical and social intelligence, such as use of the community and home-living skills. The current definition emphasizes the degree of skill because this is most closely linked to the need for services. Furthermore, this emphasis reflects the idea that successful functioning depends more on what one actually does than on what one is capable of doing. The adaptive skills listed in the current definition are those that most often necessitate the provision of services in order to optimize the present functioning of the individual in the community. The current definition emphasizes that determination of limitations in adaptive skills must be documented relative to age-appropriate community environments. This reflects the relativity of significance of these limitations, as already noted. The emphasis on community environments also reinforces the concept that individuals function in a social context, and it is this aspect of mental retardation that is most closely linked to the need for services. The definition of *community environment* is found in chapter 8.

AGE OF ONSET

The current definition continues the AAMR's emphasis on the developmental period as the time in which mental retardation is initially manifested. Thus, an individual with socially typical mental functioning who sustains a brain injury after the developmental period, and whose subsequent functioning is deficient in both intellectual and adaptive capabilities, is not considered to have mental retardation. On the other hand, an individual who develops typically and then sustains a significant developmental regression for any reason prior to age 18 years may considered to have mental retardation.[1]

The developmental period can be conceptualized as the period of the life cycle prior to adulthood. In Erikson's (1950) description of the life cycle, adulthood represents achievement of basic trust, autonomy, initiative, industry, identity, and intimacy. Individuals achieve these tasks at different ages, and indeed it is probably untrue to say that anyone "achieves" any one of them overnight. Rather, they are gradual, overlapping processes of psychosocial growth and development that proceed at varying rates. Mental retardation is manifested initially during the time in which these developmental processes are occurring, which is what distinguishes it from conditions arising after adulthood has been achieved. This concept derives from knowledge of brain development and cognitive development.

Many of the most critical aspects of brain development occur before birth, including the formation of neurons, selective cell death, and development of neurotransmitter systems. Glial cell development and myelin formation continue after birth as well. Much of the bulk growth of the brain is completed by approximately age 7, with further growth consisting primarily of elaboration of synapses and refining of functional connectivity. Adverse influences (such as malnutrition) occurring during this time of brain growth and development may alter the ultimate structure and function of the brain. As long as the potential for continued growth exists, however, compensatory processes may occur to counteract these adverse influences and improve ultimate structure and function. These compensatory processes likely include the effects of therapeutic interventions or services.

As brain development becomes better understood through continuing research, more prescriptive interventions will likely become available to direct these compensatory processes in a highly specific way. The net result of these genetic and developmental alterations and compensatory processes and interventions, once adulthood is achieved, is a brain that differs in structure and/or function from that of people without mental retardation. This is most clearly shown in "organic" conditions such as Down syndrome but may also exist in conditions where the etiology and pathophysiology are less well-understood (Coulter, 1987; Kavanagh, 1988; Pueschel and Mulick, 1990). By comparison, the brain of a person who grows to adulthood in a typical way reacts differently to injury once these neurodevelopmental processes are largely completed. Thus, the functional limitations observed in such individuals may "look like" mental retardation in a behavioral sense but likely differ in important aspects regarding their origin in injured brain structure and/or altered brain function. In a sense, it is comparable to the difference between a poorly built house and a well-built house that is damaged by fire. Both function poorly, but for very different reasons.

Mental retardation also reflects alterations in the process of cognitive growth and development. According to the similar structures, similar sequences hypothesis, persons with mental retardation (particular those with "nonorganic" causes) differ from other persons primarily in the rate of cognitive growth and in the level of cognitive functioning ultimately achieved (Zigler and Hodapp, 1986). Piaget's (1952) stage of abstract thinking or formal operations typically develops during adolescence, but persons with mental retardation usually do not attain this level of cognitive development (Grossman, 1983). Thus, the cognitive functioning of adults with mental retardation likely differs from that of adults with typical cognitive development. Cognitive limitations that appear after brain injury in adults with previously typical functioning may coexist with elements of their previous level of function, which would likely result in a different cognitive pattern than that of adults whose cognitive limitations began in childhood.

These considerations yield different and inexact "cutoff" points for the age at which the developmental period ends. The 1959 AAMR definition of mental retardation (Heber, 1959) noted that the upper age limit of the developmental period cannot be precisely specified. From the point of view of psychosocial development, adulthood may be achieved any time between approximately ages 15 to 25. From the point of view of brain development, most of the brain's growth and adult structure is completed by age 7. From the point of view of cognitive development, adult (abstract) thinking usually emerges during adolescence. In the current definition of mental retardation, the cutoff is set somewhat arbitrarily at age 18 because this generally corresponds to the end of high school education in the United States and is a time when many persons assume adult roles. One could argue that the cutoff age for the end of the developmental period and the beginning of adulthood may be relative to the social, cultural, and ethnic milieu and, thus, may differ in other societies. If one pursues this argument, the critical consideration would be whether the individual was functioning as an adult in that society prior to the onset of the observed cognitive and adaptive limitations. If so, then the diagnosis would be adult brain injury. If not, then the diagnosis of mental retardation would be possible.

The cutoff age of 18 years for a diagnosis of mental retardation need not cause confusion with the cutoff age of 22 years for eligibility for services under The Developmental Disabilities Act. Eligibility for services may reflect the existence of any of a variety of possible diagnoses. Mental retardation is only one diagnosis that may result in a developmental disability. Traumatic brain injury that occurs after age 18 but before age 22 may be another (different) diagnosis that may also result in a developmental disability. It is not necessary to define traumatic brain injury at ages 18 to 22 as mental retardation in order to assure provision of services to these young adults. Furthermore, the arguments in this section support the nosologic distinction between mental retardation manifested before age 18 and traumatic brain injury that occurs after age 18 but before age 22.

DURATION

Mental retardation begins prior to age 18 but may not be of lifelong duration. This is not a new concept. The decrease in prevalence of mental retardation after adolescence (e.g., Mercer, 1973) reflects the relativity of significance of the person's limitations to the social and cultural environment in adulthood. Intellectual functioning is fairly stable from childhood onward, and limitations in intellectual functioning (low IQ) in most cases are not likely to change much beyond that point. The *impact* of these limitations on functioning may change, however. If measurement of the person's level of functioning on all of the adaptive skills indicates performance that is not significantly subaverage (see chapter 4), either as the result of personal growth or of change in the demands of the environment (for example, leaving school may decrease the demand for functional academic skills), then adaptive limitations may no longer exist. If adaptive limitations no longer exist, then mental retardation is no longer a correct diagnosis. *If the individual still requires the provision of any supports or services in order to maintain functioning within the typical range, however, mental retardation should be considered to persist.* Needed supports or services may include programs available to people who do not have mental retardation (such as Social Security or accessible housing) as well as programs specifically intended for people with mental retardation. Thus, eligibility for continued services because of a diagnosis of mental retardation cannot be denied because receipt of such supports or services is assisting the individual to function well in the community. Mental retardation disappears only when the individual is able to function well in the community without any additional supports or services beyond those provided to all citizens of the community (such as police and fire protection).

This concept has interesting and important theoretical implications. If one changes the environment in such a way that the person with intellectual limitations can now function in a typical way, without the need for additional supports, might this not be a "cure" of mental retardation? Is a person with mental retardation cured by moving to such a social or cultural setting? Such an environment must be a true integrated community with a diversity of skill levels in persons of comparable age to the person with intellectual limitations. Thus, a segregated facility or setting composed only of persons with cognitive limitations, in which adaptive limitations are not manifested due to the provision of care-taking services, is not a curative environment. On the other hand, if a fully integrated society were to accept persons with intellectual limitations as equal members, and if social interdependence and productivity within this society were possible without the need for additional supports, might this not be a curative setting? Such an environment evokes Blatt's (1987) concept of the "conquest" of mental retardation through a change in social attitudes and behavior. The development of model societies of this type and sociological analysis of such communities will be a challenge.

This concept of cure also carries within it the possibility of relapse, should the capabilities of the individual or the demands of the environment change. As described earlier, mental retardation is a definition of present functioning rather than a permanent state of being, and functioning typically varies during the course of one's life. Depending on the person's adaptive skills and the occurrence of variable adjustment demands during the life cycle, a person with intellectual limitations may (in theory at least) move in and out of the constraints of the definition of mental retardation. For some individuals, mental retardation might possibly act like a remitting and relapsing condition, the existence of which would depend at any point in time on the occurrence of these demands and the person's response to them. One should keep in mind that most intellectual limitations may be lifelong, so the possibility of relapse is also lifelong. A person who was able to "walk away" from a diagnostic label of mental retardation because supports were not needed to function well in the community may need to return to the diagnosis later if continued good functioning requires the provision of supports. Anyone who has ever met the criteria for the definition of mental retardation is probably always at risk for significant functional limitations. This has important implications for legal entitlement and eligibility for services, which should logically also be lifelong.

PERSPECTIVE

This chapter is intended to ground the meaning of the current definition of mental retardation in a theoretical framework. The AAMR introduces this approach in its manual in order to emphasize the importance of such theoretical considerations to understanding the meaning of the definition. This theoretical framework is not intended to be the "last word" on the subject. Rather, it should be considered a statement of current thinking at this point in time. As such, it is intended to guide the further development of concepts about mental retardation. Many of the ideas expressed in this chapter warrant further elaboration, model-building, and empirical validation. We anticipate that further research and thinking will result in necessary changes in the framework as presented here.

---

[1]To diagnose and classify individuals with developmental regression prior to age 18, the following codes should be used. According to the multidimensional classification system described in chapter 3, if individuals meet the requirements of this definition prior to age 18, then mental retardation should be diagnosed on Dimension I. If there has been a developmental regression (such as that caused by a degenerative brain disease), "dementia" should be indicated on Dimension III and the specific etiology should be indicated, if it is known. This approach conforms to that specified in DSM-III-R (1987, p. 105).

PART II

DIAGNOSIS AND CLASSIFICATION DIMENSIONS

CHAPTER 3

DIAGNOSIS AND SYSTEMS OF SUPPORTS

Any system by which a person is diagnosed as having mental retardation and classified according to some level consists of a series of formalized rules specifying the characteristics that a person needs to possess in order to be so diagnosed and classified. Over the years, these rules have changed in response to consumer, professional, and political/social forces. Major changes in recent years have included formally incorporating the concept of adaptive behavior as part of the definition, lowering the IQ cutoff to two standard deviations below the mean on a standardized test of general intelligence, extending the upper age limit (to 18) for initial diagnosis, and focusing on appropriate environments and needed supports of the person (Landesman and Ramey, 1989; Middleton, Keene, and Brown, 1990; Seltzer, 1983).

THE MULTIDIMENSIONAL APPROACH

The 1992 definition of mental retardation is based on a multidimensional approach. This approach allows for an accurate description of change over time as well as evaluating individual responses to present growth, environmental changes, educational activities, and therapeutic interventions. The intent of the multidimensional approach is to:

* Broaden conceptualization of mental retardation
* Avoid reliance on IQ to assign a level of disability
* Relate the individual's needs to appropriate levels of supports

This intent is accomplished by focusing on the following four dimensions throughout the Definition, Classification, and Systems of Supports process:

Dimension I:	Intellectual Functioning and Adaptive Skills
Dimension II:	Psychological/Emotional Considerations
Dimension III:	Physical/Health/Etiology Considerations
Dimension IV:	Environmental Considerations

From the viewpoint of the individual, a multidimensional approach requires that a comprehensive description of a person with mental retardation include:

* The existence of mental retardation (as opposed to other disabling conditions)
* A consideration of the person's psychological, emotional, health, and physical strengths and weaknesses
* A consideration of the person's current living, school/work, and community environments that facilitate or restrict quality factors
* The optimal environment and systems of supports that facilitate the person's independence/interdependence, productivity, and community integration
* A profile of needed supports based on the above factors

This chapter contains an outline for a 3-step procedure for diagnosing, classifying, and determining the needed supports of a person with mental retardation. The three steps are summarized in Figure 3.1.

FIGURE 3.1   The Three-Step Process: Diagnosis, Classification, and Systems of Supports

Dimension I: *Intellectual* *Functioning* *and Adaptive* *Skills*	**STEP 1. Diagnosis of Mental Retardation** *Determines Eligibility for Supports* Mental retardation is diagnosed if : 1. The individual's intellectual functioning is approximately 70 to 75 or below. 2. There are significant disabilities in two or more adaptive skill areas. 3. The age of onset is below 18.
Dimension II: *Psychological/* *Emotional* *Considerations* *Dimension III:* *Physical /Health/* *Etiology* *Considerations* *Dimension IV:* *Environmental* *Considerations*	**STEP 2. Classification and Description** *Identifies Strengths & Weaknesses and the Need for Supports* 1. Describe the individual's strengths and weaknesses in reference to psychological/emotional considerations. 2. Describe the individual's overall physical health and indicate the condition's etiology. 3. Describe the individual's current environmental placement and the optimal environment that would facilitate his/her continued growth and development.
	STEP 3. Profile and Intensities of Needed Supports *Identifies Needed Supports* Identify the kind and intensities of supports needed for each of the four dimensions. 1. Dimension I: Intellectual Functioning and Adaptive Skills 2. Dimension II: Psychological/Emotional Considerations 3. Dimension III: Physical Health/Etiology Considerations 4. Dimension IV: Environmental Considerations

The 1992 AAMR Definition, Classification, and Systems of Supports represents a significant departure from the previous system in that: (a) a single diagnostic code of mental retardation is used if the person meets the three criteria of age of onset, significantly subaverage abilities in intellectual functioning, and limitations in two or more adaptive skill areas; (b) the person's strengths and weaknesses are described in reference to psychological, physical, and environmental dimensions; and (c) a profile is developed of needed supports across the four dimensions of intellectual functioning and adaptive skills (Dimension I), psychological and emotional considerations (Dimension II), physical/health/etiology considerations (Dimension III), and environmental considerations (Dimension IV). *The intent of this three-step process is to broaden the conceptualization of mental retardation, to avoid reliance on IQ scores to assign a level of disability, and to relate the person's needs to the intensities of supports necessary to enhance the person's independence/interdependence, productivity, and community integration.*

STEP 1: DIAGNOSIS OF MENTAL RETARDATION

A valid diagnosis of mental retardation is based on three criteria reflecting intellectual functioning level, adaptive skill level, and chronological age at onset.

1. *Intellectual functioning level.* This part of the classification system does not change significantly from the 1983 system (Grossman, 1983). For functioning, the principal measure is the intelligence quotient (IQ) as derived from a standardized intelligence test. If a standardized measure of intelligence is available that is appropriate for the individual's cultural, linguistic, and social background, this determination is made on the basis of an IQ of approximately 70 to 75 or below. If appropriate standardization measures are not available (as, for example, in some developing countries or when persons from other countries are observed in cultural settings different from their home countries), this determination should reflect a level of performance that is lower than that observed in approximately 97 percent of persons of comparable backgrounds.

As discussed more fully in chapter 4, the assessment of intellectual functioning must involve use of a reliable, valid, and standardized individual intelligence test and be conducted by a competent, well-trained person, under favorable circumstances, and on an individual basis. *Under no circumstances should a group test of intelligence be the sole determinant of IQ for a diagnosis of retardation.*

2. *Adaptive skill level.* The second criterion is that the subaverage intellectual functioning is accompanied by related limitations in adaptive behavior. Because the application of the definition stresses that specific adaptive limitations often coexist with strengths in other adaptive skill areas, the existence of limitations in adaptive skills must be documented within the context of community environments typical of the individual's age peers and indexed to the person's individualized needs for support. In addition, a valid determination of a person's adaptive skill level requires the user of an adaptive skill assessment to evaluate the person's adaptive skill profile on an appropriately normed and standardized instrument. Such a profile reflects the person's strengths and weaknesses across representative adaptive skill areas.

3. *Age of onset.* The third criterion requires the documentation that the condition of mental retardation manifests prior to age 18, which is defined operationally as the period of time between conception and the 18th birthday. The rationale for using age 18 was discussed more fully in chapter 2.

Figure 3.2 illustrates the format to be followed in completing Step 1.

STEP 2: CLASSIFICATION AND DESCRIPTION

Once the person has been diagnosed (Step 1), then it is necessary in Step 2 to describe the person's strengths and weaknesses across the four dimensions. A format that facilitates this process is presented in Figure 3.3.

STEP 3: PROFILE AND INTENSITIES OF NEEDED SUPPORTS

As a general rule, the person's level of needed habilation and supports parallels the individual's limitations. Thus, Step 3 requires the interdisciplinary team to determine the general intensities of needed supports across the four dimensions (intellectual functioning and adaptive skills, psychological/emotional considerations, physical/ health/etiology considerations, and environmental considerations). The four possible intensities of needed supports are defined in Table 3.1.

TABLE 3.1 Definition and Examples of Intensities of Supports

Intermittent
Supports on an "as needed basis." Characterized by episodic nature, person not always needing the support(s), or short-term supports needed during life-span transitions (e.g., job loss or an acute medical crisis). Intermittent supports may be high or low intensity when provided.
Limited
An intensity of supports characterized by consistency over time, time-limited but not of an intermittent nature, may require fewer staff members and less cost than more intense levels of support (e.g., time-limited employment training or transitional supports during the school to adult provided period).
Extensive
Supports characterized by regular involvement (e.g., daily) in at least some environments (such as work or home) and not time-limited (e.g., long-term support and long-term home living support).
Pervasive
Supports characterized by their constancy, high intensity; provided across environments; potential life-sustaining nature. Pervasive supports typically involve more staff members and intrusiveness than do extensive or time-limited supports.

Identifying the profile and intensities of the person's needed supports requires an awareness of environmental demands and potential systems of supports (Baumeister, 1987). For example, many limitations can be overcome by using systems of supports that include people, prosthetics, and/or environmental accommodation (see chapter 9). In a similar manner, by relating a person's functional limitations to the intensities of needed supports, education and habilitation personnel can use behavioral descriptors associated with the respective skill areas as objectives in the development and implementation of the person's individual plan. A format for summarizing the needed supports and their intensities for each dimension is presented in Figure 3.4.

FIGURE 3.2 Step 1: Diagnosis of Mental Retardation

AAMR Diagnosis, Classification, and Systems of Supports

STEP 1. DIAGNOSIS OF MENTAL RETARDATION

Name_____ Date_____ DOB_____

Team Members _____   _____

                                                _____

1. IQ_____ Test Administered_____ Date_____

2. Related limitations in two or more adaptive skill areas
   ❏ Yes ❏ No

Adaptive Evaluations_____Date_____; _____ Date _____

SIGNIFICANT LIMITATION

	YES	NO		YES	NO
Communication	❏	❏	Self-direction	❏	❏
Self-care	❏	❏	Health & safety	❏	❏
Home living	❏	❏	Functional academics	❏	❏
Social skills	❏	❏	Leisure	❏	❏
Community use	❏	❏	Work	❏	❏

3. Age of onset_____

4. Diagnosis_____

Diagnosis of mental retardation if:
- The person's intellectual functioning level is approximately 70 to 75 or below,
- There are related limitations in two or more applicable adaptive skill areas, and
- The age of onset is 18 or below.

Guidelines: Intellectual Assessment
1. The determination of subaverage intellectual functioning requires the use of global measures that include different types of items and different factors of intelligence. The instruments more commonly used include The Stanford-Binet Intelligence Scale, one of the Wechsler scales (WISC-III, WAIS-R), or the Kaufman Assessment Battery for Children.
2. If a valid IQ is not possible, significantly subaverage intellectual capabilities means a level of performance that is less than that observed in the vast majority (approximately 97 percent) of persons of comparable background.
3. In order to be valid, the assessment of cognitive performance must be free from errors caused by motor, sensory, emotional, or cultural factors.

Guidelines: Adaptive Behavior
1. Adaptive skill assessment instruments should be used that are normed within the community environments on individuals who are the same age grouping as the individual being evaluated.
2. Validity can be increased through techniques such as reviewing case histories, interviewing key people in the individual's life, observing the individual in his/her environment, interviewing the individual directly, or interacting with him/her in their daily routine.

FIGURE 3.3 Step 2: Classification and Description

STEP 2. CLASSIFICATION & DESCRIPTION

Name_____ Date_____

Dimension I: Intellectual Functioning & Adaptive Skills

Describe the individual's strengths and weaknesses in intellectual functioning and adaptive behavior based on testing or observation. Indicate source.

- **Communication**

Strengths	
	Source
Weaknesses	
	Source

- **Self-Care**

Strengths	
	Source
Weaknesses	
	Source

- **Home Living**

Strengths	
	Source
Weaknesses	
	Source

FIGURE 3.3 (continued)

- **Social Skills**

Strengths	
	Source
Weaknesses	
	Source

- **Community Use**

Strengths	
	Source
Weaknesses	
	Source

- **Self-Direction**

Strengths	
	Source
Weaknesses	
	Source

- **Health & Safety**

Strengths	
	Source
Weaknesses	
	Source

- **Functional Academics**

Strengths	
	Source
Weaknesses	
	Source

FIGURE 3.3 (continued)

- **Leisure**

Strengths	
	Source
Weaknesses	
	Source

- **Work**

Strengths	
	Source
Weaknesses	
	Source

Dimension II: Psychological/Emotional Considerations

Describe the individual's strengths and weaknesses using behavioral observations, clinical assessments, or formal diagnosis (e.g., DSM-III-R). Indicate source.

Strengths	
	Source
Weaknesses	
	Source

Dimension III: Physical/Health/Etiology Considerations

List health related diagnosis, primary etiology, and contributing factors based on behavioral observation, clinical assessment, or formal diagnosis (e.g., ICD 9).

Health related diagnosis_____

_____

_____

Primary etiology _____

Contributing factors_____

_____

_____

FIGURE 3.4   Step 3: Profile and Intensities of Needed Supports

STEP 3. PROFILE & INTENSITIES OF NEEDED SUPPORTS

Name_____   Date_____

List the support function, the specific activity, and the level of intensities needed in each of the areas and/or dimensions.

Levels of intensity are: I - Intermittent; L- Limited; E- Extensive; P- Pervasive

Dimension I: Intellectual Functioning & Adaptive Skills

Dimension/Area	Support Function	Activity	Level of Intensity I L E P
Communication			
Self-Care			
Social Skills			
Home Living			
Community Use			
Self-Direction			
Health & Safety			

FIGURE 3.4 (continued)

Dimension I: Intellectual Functioning & Adaptive Skills *(continued)*

Dimension/Area	Support Function	Activity	Level I L E P
Functional Academics			
Leisure			
Work			

Dimension II: Psychological/Emotional Considerations

Dimension/Area	Support Function	Activity	Level I L E P

Dimension III: Physical/Health Considerations

Dimension/Area	Support Function	Activity	Level I L E P

Dimension IV: Environmental Considerations

Dimension/Area	Support Function	Activity	Level I L E P

Figure 3.4 (continued)

Dimension IV: Environmental Considerations

Describe the extent to which the individual's living, work and educational environments **facilitate** or **restrict** opportunities for community integration, social supports (family and friends), and material well-being (income, housing, possessions).

- **Living Situations**

Strengths
Source
Weaknesses
Source

- **Work**

Strengths
Source
Weaknesses
Source

- **Educational**

Strengths
Source
Weaknesses
Source

Optimal Environment

Describe the optimal environment that would facilitate the individual's **independence/ interdependence, productivity,** and **community integration.**

IMPLICATIONS OF THE CLASSIFICATION SYSTEM

The Definition, Classification, and Systems of Supports just described contains a number of concepts that, when implemented, will have significant implications for the current mental retardation service delivery system. The primary implication relates to the elements of mental retardation and the intensities of needed supports. First, the use of a single diagnostic code of mental retardation removes the previous, largely IQ-based labels of mild, moderate, severe, and profound. The person either is diagnosed as having or not having mental retardation based upon meeting the three criteria of age of onset and significantly subaverage abilities in intellectual functioning and two or more adaptive skill areas.

The concept of needed supports reflects the contemporary perspective regarding the expectation for growth and potential of people; focus on personal choice, opportunity, and autonomy; and the need for people to be both in and of the community. This step applies the zero reject model in which all persons are given the supports necessary to enhance their independence/interdependence, productivity, and community integration.

The system also reflects the reality that many persons with mental retardation do not have limitations in all adaptive skill areas and, therefore, do not need supports in those unaffected areas. This part of the system also changes the focus of service delivery from a maintenance orientation to one that stresses personal growth and development. In this regard, there are important similarities between the new classification system and the current definition of developmental disabilities found in the Developmental Disabilities Act Amendments of 1984. First is the emphasis in both systems on multiple areas of functional limitations and the need for an extended array of long-term services from a multiplicity of service providers, not on a specific category (such as mental retardation). Second, the determination of functional limitations for a particular person is a clinical determination and does not depend simply on the person's label. Third, both approaches attempt to link planning, service provision, and eligibility determination to the person's capability level, not to a categorical label.

A final implication of the new system relates to terminology. As discussed previously, terms such as *mildly*, *moderately*, *severely*, or *profoundly retarded* will no longer be used. Thus, a diagnosis might well be "a person with mental retardation who needs limited supports in communication and social skills." Another sample diagnosis might be "a person with mental retardation with extensive supports needed in the areas of social skills and self-direction." Such descriptions are more functional, relevant, and oriented to service delivery and outcomes than the labeling system currently in use.

In summary, the purpose of the three-step approach to Definition, Classification, and Systems of Supports described in this chapter is to provide a detailed description of the individual and his or her needed supports. This permits recognition of all separate areas of need that may require intervention while recognizing their interdependence. It also facilitates the design of treatment approaches or service delivery plans that take into account all aspects of the person's functioning. From the viewpoint of the individual, it permits a more accurate description of change over time, including individual responses to personal growth, environmental changes, educational activities, and therapeutic intervention. Finally, it focuses on the potential of one's environment to provide the services and supports that will enhance the person's opportunities for personal life satisfaction.

CHAPTER 4

DIMENSION I: INTELLECTUAL FUNCTIONING AND ADAPTIVE SKILLS

Our purpose in this chapter is to describe assessment practices relevant to Dimension I of the Definition, Classification, and Systems of Supports for mental retardation. Assessment practices in this dimension focus on intellectual functioning and adaptive skills. Limitations in adaptive skills may often be associated with living environments or lack of social supports. The individual need not have difficulty in all of the listed areas, but at least two limitations in adaptive skills must exist. Indeed, some of these adaptive skills may constitute relative or absolute strengths for an individual identified as having mental retardation. Subsequent chapters address assessment issues within the dimensions of psychological/emotional considerations (Dimension II), physical/health/etiology considerations (Dimension III), and environmental considerations (Dimension IV).

The initial purpose of assessment is to ascertain a representative level of functioning relative to the general population on the dimensions of intellectual functioning and adaptive skills in order to determine initial or continuing eligibility for school or community services. When adaptive skills are more precisely assessed, these results also can contribute to the identification of programming goals and objectives and to specific program development. In the discussion that follows, primary attention is given to conceptualizations, measurement criteria, and available measures and assessment issues relevant to the measurement of intellectual functioning and adaptive skills.

INTELLECTUAL FUNCTIONING

The first dimension within the concept of mental retardation requires the existence of significantly subaverage intellectual functioning. Assessment data should be reported by an examiner(s) experienced with people who have mental retardation and qualified in terms of professional and state regulations as well as publisher's guidelines to conduct a thorough, valid psychological examination of the individual's conceptual intelligence. In some instances, this may require an interdisciplinary evaluation. Assuming that appropriate standardized measures are available for the individual's social, linguistic, and cultural background, and that proper adaptations may be made for any motor or sensory limitation, the conceptual intelligence criterion of performance should be approximately two or more standard deviations below the mean. This criterion assumes a standard score of approximately 70 to 75 or below on scales with a mean of 100 and standard deviation of 15. Although reliance on an IQ standard score presents a series of concerns (discussed later), it is currently the only way to address the intellectual aspect of mental retardation in a normative way. If appropriate standardized measures of conceptual intelligence are not available (as, for example, in some developing countries, or when persons are observed in cultural settings different from their home countries), the general guideline for consideration of intellectual functioning performance as determined by clinical judgment is that it must be below the level attained by approximately 97 percent of persons of comparable age and cultural backgrounds. As further research in this area is reported, a greater degree of precision may be able to be applied to this area of concern.

This manual reaffirms the practice advocated in the 1983 AAMR manual of a ceiling of approximately 70 to 75. This range acknowledges the importance of potential measurement error in the assessment instrument being used. It further affirms the importance of professional judgment in individual cases. It also represents concurrence with the need to move away from the rigid use of standard deviations in determining a ceiling for mental retardation (Kidd, 1984; Polloway, 1985) because such standards imply a degree of precision in measurement and construct that is not warranted. Although an IQ range of approximately 70 to 75 or below remains somewhat arbitrary, it nevertheless has practical benefits, among which are its general familiarity and acceptance by professionals (Zigler, Balla, and Hodapp, 1984) and its consistency with laws and regulations both within and outside the United States (e.g., Frankenberger and Harper, 1988).

The determination that an individual's intellectual functioning is significantly below the mean fulfills the first requirement for being diagnosed as having mental retardation. This criterion, consistent with the most recent manual (Grossman, 1983), is retained within the current definition and classification procedure to reaffirm the importance of the intellectual component of mental retardation. Conceptual intelligence usually is measured with standardized, psychological tests administered by appropriately trained professionals. The American Psychological Association, American Educational Research Association, and other major societies have published standards that require test publishers to specify the qualifications a person must have in order to administer any given test of intelligence.

The results of intelligence tests provide only one part of an overall assessment of intelligence. Further evaluation and professional judgment are necessary to determine when an IQ standard score is, or is not, valid for a given individual. The individual's intellectual functioning in everyday settings and roles must be consistent with the performance on the standardized measures. Test scores without confirmation from an individual's functioning in the context of age, setting, and environment can generally not be accepted as sufficient for the diagnosis of significant subaverage intellectual functioning.

THE NATURE OF IQ

Individual intelligence tests yield a standard score that can be used as a working measure suggesting a range of conceptual intelligence. As adapted from Grossman (1983, p. 31), salient aspects of an IQ (as derived from instruments with a standard deviation of 15) are summarized as follows:

1. An IQ of 100 is the mean, median, and mode of appropriately selected normative groups. Hence, a person receiving a standard score of 100 is considered to have an average level of cognitive functioning.

2. About one half of scores are between 90 and 110. This is often said to indicate the range of "average" intelligence.

3. About two thirds of the scores are between one standard deviation below the mean of 100 and one standard deviation above the mean. Hence, assuming the standard deviation of 15 points common to many instruments, two thirds of IQs would be expected to lie between 85 and 115, one sixth below 85, and one sixth above 115. These percentages illustrate the concept of the normal distribution of intelligence.

4. About 2.3 percent of IQs would be expected to lie below 70 and a like percent above 130. Thus, to delimit the diagnosis of mental retardation to people with IQs of approximately 70 to 75 or below is to suggest that hypothetically about 3 to 5 percent of the tested population may have significantly subaverage general intellectual functioning. However, as the definition clearly states, and as discussion later in this chapter explains, low IQ standard scores alone are not sufficient for diagnosis.

The determination of subaverage intellectual functioning requires the use of global measures that include different types of items and different factors of intelligence (Reschly, 1987). The instruments most commonly used for the assessment of intellectual functioning are the Stanford-Binet Intelligence Scale (Thorndike, Hagen, and Sattler, 1986), one of the Wechsler scales (e.g., the Wechsler Intelligence Scale for Children-III [Wechsler, 1991]; Wechsler Adult Intelligence Scale-Revised [Wechsler, 1981]; Wechsler Preschool and Primary Scale of Intelligence [Wechsler, 1967]), and the Kaufman Assessment Battery for Children (K-ABC, Kaufman and Kaufman, 1983).

SPECIAL CONSIDERATIONS IN ASSESSMENT OF INTELLECTUAL FUNCTIONING

The assessment of intellectual functioning through the primary reliance on intelligence tests is fraught with the potential for misuse if consideration is not given to possible errors in measurement. An obtained IQ standard score must always be considered in terms of the accuracy of its measurement. Because all measurement, and particularly psychological measurement, has some potential for error, obtained scores may actually represent a range of several points. This variation around a hypothetical "true score" may be hypothesized to be due to relatively small variations in test performance, examiner's behavior, or other undetermined factors. Variance in scores may or may not represent changes in the individual's actual or true level of functioning. Errors of measurement as well as true changes in performance outcome must be considered in the interpretations of test results. This process is facilitated by considering the concept of standard error of measurement, which has been estimated to be three to five points for well-standardized measures of general intellectual functioning. This means that if an individual is retested with the same instrument, the second obtained score would be within one standard error of measurement (i.e., +3 to 5 IQ points) of the first estimates about two thirds of the time. Thus, an IQ standard score is best seen as bounded by a range that would approximate 3 to 5 points above and below the obtained score. This range can best be considered as a "zone of uncertainty" (Reschly, 1987). Therefore, an IQ of 70 is most accurately understood not as a precise score, but as a range of confidence with parameters of at least one standard error, that is, scores of about 66 to 74 (2/3 probability) or parameters of two standard errors, that is, scores of 62 to 78 (95/100 probability) (Grossman, 1983). This is a critical consideration that must be part of any decision concerning a diagnosis of mental retardation.

Another important source of possible variation lies in test content differences across different scales and between different age levels on the same scale. For example, scores determined on verbal tests, such as from the Wechsler Verbal scale, frequently differ from those obtained on nonverbal tests (e.g., the Wechsler Performance scale). Variations also may be attributed to differences in the standardization samples, to changes between different editions of the same scale, to shifts to an alternative scale as an individual's chronological age increases, and to variances in the person's abilities or performance. Finally, variances in scores between successive revisions of intelligence measures have also been noted (Evans, 1991).

Intertest differences tend to result in greater variance in measured intelligence than those attributed to measurement error associated with the use of a single scale. As with error of measurement, these variations must be carefully considered by individuals with appropriate training in order to avoid overreliance on any specific obtained score (Grossman, 1983).

ADAPTIVE SKILLS

The second consideration within the definition of mental retardation is the existence of limitations in adaptive skills. Limitations must occur in two or more applicable adaptive skills areas: communication, self-care, home living, social skills, community use, self-direction, health and safety, functional academics, leisure, and work. The general dimensions of adaptive skills correspond reasonably well to the two basic concepts that have emerged from research on adaptive behavior: personal independence and social responsibility (Bruininks and McGrew, 1987; Bruininks, Thurlow, and Gilman, 1987; McGrew and Bruininks, 1989). The requirement of two or more adaptive skill limitations reflects the fact that impact on functioning must be sufficiently apparent to show a generalized disability. In addition, the inclusion of two areas reduces the probability of diagnostic error that could occur from the minimal requirement of only one disability, a finding that might be common to a large number of individuals.

The concept of adaptive skills is a continuation of the traditional historical attention given to social competence in the diagnosis of mental retardation, a precursor to the term *adaptive behavior*. Adaptive skills is an outgrowth of the concept of adaptive behavior, which was first formally included in the 1959 definition (Heber, 1959) and was defined in Grossman (1983) as follows:

> Adaptive behavior refers to the quality of everyday performance in coping with environmental demands. The quality of general adaptation is mediated by level of intelligence; thus, the two concepts overlap in meaning. It is evident, however, from consideration of the definition of adaptive behavior, with its stress on everyday coping, that adaptive behavior refers to what people do to take care of themselves and to relate to others in daily living rather than the abstract potential implied by intelligence. (p. 42)

The focus on the term *adaptive skills* is not intended as a refutation of the term *adaptive behavior*. Rather, it represents a change due in part to the concern surrounding the conceptual nature of adaptive behavior and the ensuing issues related to measurement. One can argue that adaptive behavior has become conceptually allied to the content of commercial adaptive behavior scales. Thus, for example, if a scale measures only out-of-school domains, the concept of adaptive behavior becomes focused only on this environment to the exclusion of in-school factors, thus creating a noncomprehensive view of adaptive skills (Reschly, 1990).

The concept of adaptive skills implies an array of competencies and, thus, provides a firmer foundation in several of the definition's key statements; that is, adaptive skill limitations often coexist with strengths in other adaptive skills or other areas of personal competence, and the existence of these limitations and strengths in adaptive skills must be both documented within the context of community environments typical of the individual's age peers and tied to the person's individualized needs for support. It further emphasizes that if an individual does not have adaptive skill limitations, then the diagnosis of mental retardation is not applicable.

Finally, it is important to consider Evans' (1991) description of adaptive behavior as reflecting both the ability to fit into a given niche as well as "the ability to change one's behavior to suit the demands of a situation" (p. 34). Thus, adaptive skills in an institutional setting are not suited to a normalized community setting and vice versa. An implication of these views is that the conceptualization and measurement of "maladaptive" behavior skills as being synonymous with specific acts judged as being in excess and significantly undesirable or inappropriate should be questioned (Evans, 1991). Recent research on the function of behavior problems in persons with severe disabilities (Durand and Crimmins, 1988; Durand and Kishi, 1987) demonstrates that such behavior may be an adaptation judged by others to be undesirable but often representing a response to environmental conditions and, in some cases, a lack of alternative communication skills. For this reason, the concept of maladaptive behavior is not included in Dimension I of the classification scheme and, rather, is subsumed within Dimension II.

In spite of the fact that previous definitions have indicated that intelligence and adaptive behavior should have equal weight in diagnosis, in practice IQ has typically dominated and, thus, has been overemphasized both in terms of professional decision-making and classification (e.g., Furlong and LeDrew, 1985; Harrison, 1987; Reschly and Ward, 1991) and research (e.g., Hawkins and Cooper, 1990; J. Smith and Polloway, 1978). The increased attention to adaptive skills in the current scheme is an attempt to encourage a balanced consideration of IQ and adaptive skill measures. It should also stimulate the further development and refinement of measures that have programmatic value.

The specific adaptive skill areas identified in the definition provide further clarification for the concept of adaptive behavior as discussed in the 1983 manual, where adaptive behavior was placed in the context of the developmental periods of infancy and early childhood, childhood and early adolescence, late adolescence, and adulthood. A continuing theme is the importance of the developmental relevance of specific skills within these adaptive areas. Thus, attention to specific skill areas should be given only in instances where they are age-relevant because several of the areas (e.g., work) focus on adolescence and adulthood. Specific examples of the adaptive skill areas that follow are based in part on a descriptive system developed by Ford and colleagues (Ford et al., 1989). Their use in diagnosis is discussed later in this chapter.

1. *Communication*: Skills include the ability to comprehend and express information through symbolic behaviors (e.g., spoken word, written word/orthography, graphic symbols, sign language, manually coded English) or nonsymbolic behaviors (e.g., facial expression, body movement, touch, gesture). Specific examples include the ability to comprehend and/or receive a request, an emotion, a greeting, a comment, a protest, or rejection. Higher level skills of communication (e.g., writing a letter) would also relate to functional academics.

2. *Self-Care*: skills involved in toileting, eating, dressing, hygiene, and grooming.

3. *Home-Living*: skills related to functioning within a home, which include clothing care, housekeeping, property maintenance, food preparation and cooking, planning and budgeting for shopping, home safety, and daily scheduling. Related skills include orientation and behavior in the home and nearby neighborhood, communication of choices and needs, social interaction, and application of functional academics in the home.

4. *Social*: skills related to social exchanges with other individuals, including initiating, interacting, and terminating interaction with others; receiving and responding to pertinent situational cues; recognizing feelings; providing positive and negative feedback; regulating one's own behavior; being aware of peers and peer acceptance; gauging the amount and type of interaction with others; assisting others; forming and fostering of friendships and love; coping with demands from others; making choices; sharing; understanding honesty and fairness; controlling impulses; conforming conduct to laws; violating rules and laws; and displaying appropriate socio-sexual behavior.

5. *Community Use*: skills related to the appropriate use of community resources, including traveling in the community; grocery and general shopping at stores and markets; purchasing or obtaining services from other community businesses (e.g., gas stations, repair shops, doctor and dentist's offices); attending church or synagogue; using public transportation and public facilities, such as schools, libraries, parks and recreational areas, and streets and sidewalks; attending theaters; and visiting other cultural places and events. Related skills include behavior in the community, communication of choices and needs, social interaction, and the application of functional academics.

6. *Self-Direction*: skills related to making choices; learning and following a schedule; initiating activities appropriate to the setting, conditions, schedule, and personal interests; completing necessary or required tasks; seeking assistance when needed; resolving problems confronted in familiar and novel situations; and demonstrating appropriate assertiveness and self-advocacy skills.

7. *Health and Safety*: skills related to maintenance of one's health in terms of eating; illness identification, treatment, and prevention; basic first aid; sexuality; physical fitness; basic safety considerations (e.g., following rules and laws, using seat belts, crossing streets, interacting with strangers, seeking assistance); regular physical and dental check-ups; and personal habits. Related skills include protecting oneself from criminal behavior, using appropriate behavior in the community, communicating choices and needs, participating in social interactions, and applying functional academics.

8. *Functional Academics*: cognitive abilities and skills related to learning at school that also have direct application in one's life (e.g., writing; reading; using basic practical math concepts, basic science as it relates to awareness of the physical environment and one's health and sexuality; geography; and social studies). It is important to note that the focus of this skill area is not on grade-level academic achievement but, rather, on the acquisition of academic skills that are functional in terms of independent living.

9. *Leisure*: the development of a variety of leisure and recreational interests (i.e., self-entertainment and interactional) that reflect personal preferences and choices and, if the activity will be conducted in public, age and cultural norms. Skills include choosing and self-initiating interests, using and enjoying home and community leisure and recreational activities alone and with others, playing socially with others, taking turns, terminating or refusing leisure or recreational activities, extending one's duration of participation, and expanding one's repertoire of interests, awareness, and skills. Related skills include behaving appropriately in the leisure and recreation setting, communicating choices and needs, participating in social interaction, applying functional academics, and exhibiting mobility skills.

10. *Work*: skills related to holding a part or full-time job or jobs in the community in terms of specific job skills, appropriate social behavior, and related work skills (e.g., completion of tasks; awareness of schedules; ability to seek assistance, take criticism, and improve skills; money management, financial resources allocation, and the application of other functional academic skills; and skills related to going to and from work, preparation for work, management of oneself while at work, and interaction with coworkers).

ASSESSMENT MEASURES

A variety of adaptive behavior scales were developed in the wake of the formal inclusion of adaptive behavior in earlier AAMR definitions of mental retardation. As a consequence, there is relatively close correspondence between the structure of many of the scales and the implicit meanings within those definitions (Kamphaus, 1987). Further, the wide availability of formal measures is also a logical phenomenon paralleling the attention given in the early to mid-1970s to the overrepresentation of minorities in special education programs and subsequent litigation and to the popular use of the concept of the "six hour retarded child."

The available scales differ significantly in their quality, standardization sample, and intended usage. Although some were normed only on individuals who were identified as having severe disabilities, others focused on individuals identified as having mild mental retardation. Some scales purport to measure general adaptive behavior and, thus, function primarily as a contribution to the diagnosis of mental retardation, whereas other scales offer the means to assess in depth an individual's competencies in a specific domain; thus, classification versus programming purposes can be noted. In addition, specific adaptive skill concerns, for example, in the domains of communication and social skills, are more appropriately assessed with instruments designed for those respective, specific domains rather than through reliance on general adaptive behavior scales. Consequently, not only must professionals select instruments that are technically adequate, they must also be cautious to select ones designed for the particular population, the functional purpose, and the specific adaptive skills intended (Reschly, 1990). The potential user is encouraged to employ adaptive skill assessment instruments that are normed within community environments on individuals who are of the same age grouping as the individual being evaluated. Scales normed primarily on persons experiencing segregated school, work, and living settings may have validity limited to those contexts. Finally, the user should be aware that older tests often have established credibility because any unusual results have been subject to scrutiny and correction.

For many years, the Vineland Social Maturity Scale (Doll, 1953) served as the standard measure of adaptive behavior. However, a variety of tools are now available and in common use. These instruments include the AAMD Adaptive Behavior Scales (ABS) (Nihira, Foster, Shellhaas, and Leland, 1974), the School Edition of the ABS (Lambert and Windmiller, 1981), the revised Vineland Adaptive Behavior Scales (Sparrow, Balla, and Cichetti, 1984), the Scales of Independent Behavior (Bruininks, Woodcock, Weatherman, and Hill, 1984), and the Comprehensive Test of Adaptive Behavior (Adams, 1984). For a critique of these and other instruments, readers may wish to review Reschly (1987, 1990).

USE OF ADAPTIVE SKILLS ASSESSMENT DATA

Reporting of scores. Despite increased emphasis on adaptive skills in the definition, there has been virtually no support for the use of a single global score or age equivalent index to operationalize adaptive skill limitations. Since the 1983 manual, little has changed to promote such a trend. Frankenberger and Harper (1988), for example, noted that only six states even make reference to an adaptive behavior cutoff score in their guidelines for the identification of mental retardation. There are a number of reasons why a global score and precise cutoff point would not be productive.

First, because many facets of a person's behavior are sampled in adaptive skills assessment, the reliance on a single score would result in the omission of a description of these behaviors in a daily life context. Second, because there is often within-subject variation in adaptive behavior, it is critical to report component scores in order for the assessment process to have meaning. Third, a profile of scores and/or skill descriptions has significance to the client and those responsible for designing appropriate interventions, including placement into programs and planning for services. Because single items or groups of items represent specific areas of proficiency, adaptive behavior skill profiles can be used to set priorities for training. Some scales have been specifically developed to establish intervention targets and to measure treatment outcomes (Grossman, 1983).

Assessment procedures. Few of the current measures of adaptive behavior allow assessment of the entire breadth and range of adaptive skill development found in persons with mental retardation. As Sattler (1988) stated, "no one instrument can measure all of the relevant domains of adaptive behavior" (p. 376). The further development of measures to assess both the broad range and specific areas of adaptive skills is clearly a priority in order for the current definition to be fully and properly operationalized in a manner that will enable the identification of needed supports and, thus, be beneficial to persons having mental retardation.

Additional improvements in adaptive skills measures should be focused on addressing ways to enhance the indirect or interview mode of assessment as well as to complement it with other measurement strategies. Most current assessment scales rely primarily on the recording of information obtained from a third person who is familiar with the individual being assessed. Thus, assessment typically takes the form of an interview process, with the respondent being a parent, teacher, or direct-service provider rather than reflecting direct observation of a client's adaptive behavior or from a client's self-report (Voelker et al., 1990).

Because raters are the key to obtaining valid data, it is important that they be carefully selected. Key criteria include the depth of their knowledge about the person to be evaluated (i.e., have known him or her for at least 3 months and have observed and interacted with him or her) and their willingness to cooperate on the task (i.e., they are not resentful toward their job or poorly motivated) (Reiss, 1988). Because the evaluations may be subject to the biases of the respondents, their credibility should be considered (Sattler, 1988). The use of at least two raters to score an individual on the same scale and derivation of an average of the results will increase the validity of the results because they will reflect the opinions of two persons (Reiss, 1988) and provide a check on the accuracy of an informant's responses (Keyes, 1990). In addition, supplementing interviews of service providers with direct observation can also enable more accurate assessment of an individual's adaptive skills.

Another area that warrants further attention is the use of self-reports of adaptive skills. Voelker et al. (1990) reported findings that although staff reports of maladaptive behavior always indicated more behavior problems than did self-reports elicited from the clients, adaptive behavior reports from both sources showed no significant differences. Attention to the role of self-reports highlights several concerns: (a) whether staff members exaggerate behavior problems because such behavior may complicate their jobs and (b) whether clients' behavior problems may simply be a means for communication (in settings where outlets may be limited or when clients lack alternate means to express themselves). Self-ratings nevertheless have certain disadvantages. Reiss (in press) reviewed the literature on self versus informant measures and concluded that the former had lower internal reliability, may be unduly affected by defensiveness on the part of a respondent who has mental retardation, and may have more utility for the way an individual responds versus the actual content of the response. Finally, as noted previously, bias in informant responses can be controlled in part via the averaging of ratings to yield a consensus judgment. Therefore, the primary value of self-ratings may be in providing additional data to further enhance an assessment profile.

CRITICAL ISSUES IN ASSESSMENT

General issues in the assessment of intellectual functioning and adaptive skills derive in large part from those issues that relate to measurement in any other dimension. Therefore, general concerns for validity, reliability, and, more specifically, for stability of measures, generalization, and prediction, as well as appropriateness of use, are critical in assessment of mental retardation. Although some intelligence tests currently available have been used for years, longevity alone does not validate a test's results for a specific individual. Further, many of the available adaptive behavior scales fall short of appropriate standards for norming (Kamphaus, 1987) and clarity of the construct of adaptive behavior (Evans, 1991). The continuing role of test scores derived from standardized assessment is at least a partial basis for classifying individuals as having mental retardation should underscore the importance of selecting measures that do not violate these basic technical standards.

The assessment of intellectual functioning and adaptive skills should be done only by individuals who are qualified according to professional standards, including those developed by the publishers, professional associations (e.g., the American Psychological Association), and state credentialing regulations (e.g., certification, licensure). In addition, given the justified concern expressed by both consumers and professionals that tests may be inappropriately employed in diagnosis, educational placement, and habilitation planning, certain safeguards concerning assessment in general have been enacted into state and federal law. Although the following protections relate most specifically to the educational services, they also are applicable to assessment considerations in general.

1. Assessments should be initiated only for sufficient cause. For example, referrals for assessment should be evaluated to ensure that there is adequate cause for initiating the formal assessment process.

2. The parent or guardian of a school child must give consent to an assessment and has the right to participate in and appeal any determinations made and any placement and program decisions that follow. Under some circumstances, they may also request an external assessment.

3. Assessments are to be undertaken only by fully qualified, certified, or licensed professionals under laws and regulations that govern their specialties.

4. Assessment procedures must be adjusted to account for specific deficits in hearing, vision, health, or movement and modified to accommodate those whose background, culture, or language differs from the general population upon which specific tests were standardized. Assessments should be sensitive to the environmental background of the individual.

5. Those individuals conducting assessments will refer to appropriately trained specialists any person suspected of having hearing, health, or other problems that warrant special consideration in assessment.

6. Conclusions and recommendations should be made on the basis of all information, including that derived from interviews with people acquainted with the person (including the family) and from observations of the person's behavior. Diagnosis must be multifactorial and thus not be based upon a single determinant, such as IQ.

7. Periodic reassessments must be made to confirm or correct previous judgments and to consider changes in developmental pace that may necessitate programming changes. The schedule for such assessments will typically be determined by the nature of the services being provided.

8. Individuals may exercise their right to refuse assessment procedures and thus effectively remove themselves from the diagnostic process and/or from eligibility for services.

The subsections that follow address the use of assessment data, cultural and linguistic diversity, sensory and motor impairments, and the selection of instruments.

APPROPRIATE USE OF ASSESSMENT RESULTS

The majority of the criticisms that have been leveled at intelligence tests and, to a lesser extent, adaptive behavior scales, ultimately concern appropriate use rather than instrument construction per se. It is, therefore, critical to recognize that data obtained from instruments measuring intellectual functioning or adaptive skills are intended as only one part of the overall evaluation process. Other data (as discussed later) combined with professional judgment within the context of team decision-making are necessary to determine whether the results obtained from the administration of a given measure are valid or invalid for a specific individual. Although instruments may demonstrate acceptable validity for groups, there is a possibility of substantial error in the assessment of the individual.

In order to complement the data obtained from a given measure, and thus evaluate its validity, a professional should take a number of steps. These may include:

- Arranging for subsequent administration of an instrument (e.g., an adaptive behavior rating scale) by another rater so that results can be averaged (Consensus evaluations of two or more persons tend to be more reliable than evaluations derived from only one individual [Reiss, 1988].)
- Reviewing case histories of the individual
- Interviewing key persons in the individual's life
- Observing the individual in his or her natural environment
- Interviewing the individual directly or interacting with him or her in a play or other social setting

The addition of other sources of data provides a basis for more informed professional judgment by providing a context within which to evaluate the validity of the obtained measures. This emphasis underscores the importance of clinical judgment in this process. This approach is the preferred option to the sole reliance on a single measure or test of intellectual functioning or adaptive skills and to a single evaluator or rater. It emphasizes the importance of convergent validity, that is, the consistency of information obtained from different sources and settings. The importance of such a focus is emphasized, for example, by the fact that specific adaptive skills are not sufficiently addressed by current scales. To illustrate, Gresham and Elliott (1987) noted that comprehensive social skills assessment would also require direct observations of behavior, sociometric tools, and role-plays or interviews.

The advent of judgment-based assessment signals a direction that is worthy of further attention. According to Neisworth and Bagnato (1988), judgment-based assessment involves organized clinical judgment that "collects, structures, and usually quantifies the impressions of professionals . . . about child/environment characteristics" (p. 36). DeLaurin (1990) stressed that professionals should work to enhance clinical judgment by operationalizing aspects of the process in order to overcome reliance on impressions not solely based on objective data, random review of data sources, conflicts in goals, biases of team members, or difficulties in working relationships. Further consideration of judgment-based assessment procedures has the potential to enhance the team decision-making process.

CULTURAL AND LINGUISTIC DIVERSITY ISSUES

Concerns related to the importance of cultural and linguistic variance in accurate assessment have received ample attention. This problem sometimes has been exacerbated by primary reliance on intelligence tests in diagnostic decision-making (Reschly and Ward, 1991). Rather, sensitivity to cultural and linguistic diversity clearly requires reliance on multifactorial assessment. When an individual referred for evaluation does not significantly differ from the cultural norm, evaluation is relatively straightforward. However, when his or her background reflects cultural or linguistic variances, alternate approaches should be considered. Sociocultural background as well as the individual's primary language should be considered in the selection and administration of assessment instruments and the interpretation of the results obtained from those assessment activities (Reschly, 1987). The increased emphasis on the importance of adaptive skills measures, as discussed in this manual, represents one way to reinforce the necessary trend toward increased sensitivity to cultural differences.

One approach to assessment in response to the issue of diversity is the System of Multicultural Pluralistic Assessment (SOMPA, Mercer and Lewis, 1977), briefly reviewed here for illustrative purposes only. With SOMPA, a traditional IQ is still determined, but an appropriate sociocultural normative group is also established for the individual. Thus, pluralistic norms are specifically derived by the identification of background characteristics thought to be related to intellectual performance, the determination of the relative weight of each characteristic in the prediction of performance, and the determination of a predicted score for an individual from his or her cultural background (i.e., estimated learning potential). If both IQ and estimated learning potential are low, there is no need for adjustments. However, if IQ is low while estimated learning potential (ELP) is above the cutoff for mental retardation, the SOMPA-recommended decision on the intellectual functioning dimension would be against classification. The ELP measure is then complemented by data from the Adaptive Behavior Inventory for Children (ABIC).

Such an approach offers an alternative to assessment, one that Greenspan (1990) referred to as an "ingenious strategy for protecting disadvantaged children from being victimized by the use of an IQ-only strategy for special education placement" (p. 5). It certainly focuses attention on the importance of cultural and linguistic diversity issues in assessment (Zucker and Polloway, 1987). Nevertheless, this approach may create various other problems, including the declassification of many students with mental retardation who would otherwise have been deemed eligible for services (e.g., Reschly, 1981). In addition, ELP is a nonvalidated measure suggesting that points not attained by the individual should be added to scores (Reschly, 1991). Finally, SOMPA shifts concern for bias solely toward assessment and away from the more significant issue of quality of services.

Although SOMPA may not solve the problem of equitably considering diversity concerns in assessment, it does highlight the critical issue that a diagnosis of mental retardation must take into account the sociocultural context of the individual. The key challenges are to describe important sociocultural differences and, subsequently, "to evaluate the individual's status in light of expectations and opportunities for the development of various competencies" (Reschly, 1991, p. 53). Assessments, therefore, must consider relevant ethnic or cultural standards.

SENSORY, MOTOR, AND COMMUNICATIVE DISABILITY ISSUES

Individuals who exhibit specific sensory, motor, or communicative limitations present special difficulties for accurate assessment. As a consequence, the evaluation of intellectual functioning as well as adaptive skills for an individual who may have vision, hearing, or motor impairments (e.g., related to cerebral palsy) frequently becomes a complex process (Meacham, Kline, Stovall, and Sands, 1987). For example, the assessment of individuals with hearing impairments generally requires a nonverbal instrument, whereas the assessment of persons with visual impairments requires measures that do not include object manipulation or cards or pictures (Reschly, 1987). An individual with severe motor limitations may have quite limited voluntary responses and, thus, may need to respond via an eye scan or blink. Performance measures of intelligence are particularly susceptible to misuse for individuals who have motor disabilities (e.g., cerebral palsy). Some students may exhibit multiple disabilities, thus compounding the task for the assessment specialist. In addition, as Browder and Snell (1988) noted, some individuals may simply lack "test behaviors." As a consequence, they may refuse to stay seated for the duration of an assessment session or may exhibit a high rate of stereotyped or self-stimulatory behavior. Individuals who rely on nonverbal communication may have difficulty making the requisite responses indicated for a given test. Additional problems may include fatigue, low levels of frustration, motivation, noncompliance, comprehension of instructions, drowsiness due to medication, and test anxiety (Evans, 1991; Pollingue, 1987). Finally, and significantly, a general principle is that the test results should not be unduly affected by limitations in receptive or expressive language capabilities. Such limitations may cause the test to be a measure of the problem rather than a valid assessment of intellectual functioning or adaptive skills.

The problem areas briefly noted in the preceding discussion can obviously make traditional testing procedures not feasible and could result in discriminatory assessment (Browder and Snell, 1988; Duncan, Sbardellati, Maheady, and Sainato, 1981). It is, therefore, paramount that persons charged with assessing both intellectual functioning and adaptive skills take special measures to ensure a fair and accurate evaluation. Evaluators must be able to distinguish limitations in intellectual or adaptive areas from problems associated with sensory or physical difficulties. Such persons must be prepared in the use of specialized instruments and/or modifications in existing measures. The results of intelligence testing in particular should be interpreted cautiously (Pollingue, 1987).

Many of the most commonly used instruments for the evaluation of intellectual functioning and adaptive skills have been modified for use with special populations. Meacham et al. (1987) and Pollingue (1987) discussed such modifications and suggested appropriate uses of specific adaptive behavior instruments. Due to the unique challenges in assessment that persons with multiple disabilities may present to the examiner, the specialized tests may have lower predictive validity than do, for example, the WISC-III (Wechsler, 1991) and the Stanford-Binet. As a consequence, the need should be apparent for administration and interpretation by clinicians with special expertise. In addition, assessments in such situations particularly emphasize the importance of clinical judgment in lieu of the primary reliance on obtained test scores. With further efforts to develop both appropriate instruments and assessment procedures, assessment will come to reflect actual ability and skills rather than simply the sensory disability or communicative difficulty (Meacham et al., 1987).

SELECTION OF INSTRUMENTS

The purpose of this manual is neither to identify nor endorse specific instruments that should be used for the assessment of intellectual functioning and adaptive skills. Rather, the information included herein is intended to provide some guidance for the development of procedures consistent with the Definition, Classification, and Systems of Supports for mental retardation. The section thus concludes with recommendations for potential users concerning the selection of instruments appropriate for specific assessment purposes. The following are suggestions that test users can comply with in order to become better informed about a given instrument.

1. Read the manual.

2. Determine, based on the publisher's specifications and state and professional regulations, who is properly trained to administer the instrument (e.g., instruments that require direct interaction with the client require greater expertise than rating scales completed by others, such as teachers or parents).

3. Determine that the manual is clearly written to avoid the introduction of error through confusion.

4. Ascertain that the test is accompanied by data on reliability and validity.

5. Consult with colleagues who may have familiarity with the instrument.

6. Attend seminars delivered by the author or publisher focused on training in the administration of a test or scale.

7. Ensure the accuracy of the results (e.g., determine whether scoring software has been "error-trapped" to prevent the entering of impossible answers or to control for circumstances, such as missing data, that may yield error).

8. Register with the test publisher in order to be advised of modifications or corrections.

9. Search the literature for research on its usage particularly as related to validation of its use for the particular setting, population, and purpose in question.

10. Analyze reviews in manuals such as the Mental Measurements Yearbook (Conoley & Kramer, 1989) or Tests in Print (1989).

11. Try out the test before commitment to purchase and/or widespread usage.

12. Review all components of the instrument.

13. Ensure applicability of the instrument to the population with whom you intend to use it.

New instruments that can assist with the assessment of intellectual functioning and adaptive skills are frequently developed and published. Professionals are advised to remain current with the literature in the field in order to be aware of the availability of such new instruments. At the same time, there is benefit in exercising a healthy caution toward new tools that may lack documentation of their appropriateness for use with clients. They may use current trends and popular buzz words without demonstrating that they relate to these concepts. The key point is that new instruments do not offer the advantage that established tools can; that is, exposure to careful professional scrutiny and the availability of a literature base on their validity. It is often through such scrutiny and related longevity that the credibility of a test (i.e., legal, educational, psychological) is developed.

DIAGNOSIS: USE OF DIMENSION I ASSESSMENT DATA

A diagnosis of mental retardation requires that two assessment criteria (in addition to age of onset) be met. The first is significantly subaverage intellectual functioning. This criterion serves only to assist in the determination of whether an individual is to be classified as having mental retardation but by itself is insufficient for such a diagnosis.

The second criterion for diagnosing a person as having mental retardation is that the individual have limitations in two or more adaptive skills. This part of the diagnosis is more substantive and subjective and requires clinical judgment that takes into account environmental demands and potential support systems. For example, identified limitations in many educational, vocational, and community living skills may be irrelevant if appropriate supports or prosthetics are made available or if appropriate environmental accommodations are made.

The person's adaptive skill profile must be considered in making a diagnosis of mental retardation. The general rule is that if two or more adaptive skill limitations fall substantially below the average level of functioning (as determined either by formal comparison to a normative sample or through professional judgment), then the individual would meet this second criterion for a diagnosis of mental retardation. Specifically, adaptive skills assessment can confirm a judgment of mental retardation by justifying eligibility for an individual with an IQ of approximately 70 to 75 or below who exhibits substantial limitations that interfere with independent functioning. Adaptive skills assessment should also serve to question a diagnosis of mental retardation for an individual with an IQ approximately 70 to 75 or below who has demonstrated an adequate level of adaptive functioning. Measures of adaptive skills have been seen potentially as "check[s] against excessive reliance upon measures of intelligence" (Sargent, 1981, p. 3). With the current definition, the role of adaptive skills measures needs to make an even more significant contribution. In addition, these measures constitute the basis for decision-making with regard to area and level of adaptive skills and the needs for supports and programming. By shifting to greater reliance on adaptive skills in the diagnosis of mental retardation, embedded within an orientation toward observation and clinical judgment, all persons who have significant limitations associated with the defined concept of mental retardation could be assured of eligibility for services. As Greenspan (1990) concluded:

> The challenge . . . is to become more flexible and free in assigning the
> label to persons who have a true disability . . . while being careful not to
> discriminate against persons (whether disadvantaged or not) who do not have
> a true disability. The answer is to avoid becoming wedded to scores in single
> domains (such as IQ). (pp. 31–32)

CHAPTER 5

DIMENSION II: PSYCHOLOGICAL AND EMOTIONAL CONSIDERATIONS

The multidimensional concept of mental retardation requires assessment of psychological functioning and behavior. The majority of persons evaluated under this definition will be found to be mentally healthy and free of significant behavioral problems (Menolascino, 1977). A significant minority, however, may need some type of mental health service. For these persons, the nature of the psychological or behavior problem should be noted on Dimension II of the three-step process (see Figure 3.1).

This chapter covers some of the mental health aspects of mental retardation, with a focus on adaptive and maladaptive behavior. Since the publication of the last manual (Grossman, 1983), there has been substantial broadening of perspective on maladaptive behavior to include previously neglected problems such as depression, schizophrenia, suicide, and anxiety disorders (Bruininks, Hill, and Morreau, 1988; Borthwick-Duffy and Eyman, 1990).

The coexistence of mental retardation and mental illness in the same individual presents unique diagnostic and treatment challenges to users of this manual. The major reasons for this challenge relate to the following circumstances:

- The concept of mental illness being very complex and currently poorly understood
- The lack of definitive research in this area
- The lack of consistency in the current diagnostic techniques
- The considerable amount of misunderstanding as to what constitutes mental illness in persons with mental retardation
- The inappropriate classification and definitional confusions in the past

What is known, however, is that between 20 to 35 percent of all noninstitutionalized persons with mental retardation are currently diagnosed as "mentally retarded/mentally ill" (Parsons, May, and Menolascino, 1984). Such a diagnosis has tremendous implications for both programmatic services for the person and his or her life satisfaction (Borthwick, 1988). Thus, in implementing the new definition of mental retardation with its emphasis on functionality, adaptive skill areas, environments, and appropriate supports, it is essential for the users of this manual to be sensitive to a number of considerations as they work through the steps related to diagnosis, classification, and appropriate intensities of support. In this chapter these considerations are outlined, especially as they relate to assessment and treatment issues.

CLASSIFICATION ISSUES

Cantwell and Rutter (1978) have pointed out that an adequate classification system should be (a) valid, (b) classify disorders and not persons, (c) differentiate between disorders, (d) have a developmental framework, and (e) be practical and useful. This has been the emphasis throughout this manual, and the process is described in Table 5.1 in terms of the dimensions identified in the AAMR Definition, Classification, and Systems of Supports.

TABLE 5.1 Multidimensional Classification System

Dimension		Classification
Dimension I:	Intellectual Functioning and Adaptive Skills	• Cognitive • Adaptive • Developmental
Dimension II:	Psychological/Emotional Considerations	• DSM-III-R
Dimension III:	Physical/Health/Etiology Considerations	• ICD-9 • Etiology
Dimension IV:	Environmental Considerations	• Ecological analysis

ASSESSMENT

The assessment of mental illness in persons with mental retardation is relevant to clinical research and public policy concerns. Clinicians need to assess the nature of a client's problem, identify appropriate treatments, and monitor the effects of such treatments. Researchers, on the other hand, need valid measures in order to estimate the prevalence of mental illness and study possible causes as well as develop more effective therapies for persons with mental retardation. Those involved in public policy development need accurate identification of individuals to determine who is and who is not eligible for such services and accurate epidemiological data in order to allocate resources and plan social policies.

A major concern involved in the assessment of mental illness in persons with mental retardation is the concept known as *diagnostic overshadowing* (Reiss, Levitan, and Szysko, 1982). This term refers to instances in which the presence of mental retardation decreases the diagnostic significance of an accompanying mental health disorder. For example, some of the debilitating aspects of various emotional problems may appear less significant than they really are when compared to the more debilitating effects that may be associated with mental retardation. In addition, certain types of abnormal behavior that are viewed as psychiatric disorders in persons without mental retardation may, in persons with mental retardation, as a consequence of their cognitive deficiency and not because of any evidence supporting the attribution, be considered part of the mental retardation because of the natural tendency to attribute behavior to salient factors. Further complicating the issue of assessment is that mental illness is not a single, unitary disorder but, rather, a wide range of dissimilar disorders. Moreover, there may be concern that adding the additional psychiatric diagnosis to persons who have already been identified as having mental retardation will cause further stigmatization of the person.

SOURCES OF ASSESSMENT INFORMATION

Comprehensive clinical assessment of mental illness in persons with mental retardation needs to be based upon multiple sources of information along with multidisciplinary input. Possible information sources include (a) interviews; (b) behavioral observation in everyday environments; (c) client and staff interviews; (d) formal psychometric evaluations, including social skills development, personality, and maladaptive behavior; and (e) medical and biological evaluations, including positron emission tomography and other types of neuroimaging assessment. The following is a list of instruments most regularly cited in the literature as appropriate for investigating certain aspects of psychopathology among persons with mental retardation.

- Aberrant Behavior Checklist (ABC)
- Emotional Disorders Rating Scale for Developmental Disabilities (EDRS-DD)
- Inventory for Client Agency Planning (ICAP)
- Maladaptive Behavior Rating Subscales of Adaptive Behavior Scales
- Self-Report Depression Questionnaire (SRDQ)
- The AAMR Adaptive Behavior Scales
- The Psychopathology Inventory for Mentally Retarded Adults (PIMRA)
- The Reiss Screen

There is a need for valid personality measures for persons with mental retardation. The most popular instruments used for this purpose are variants of the story-telling or apperceptive technique. However, these measures lack objectivity and require a high degree of expertise to be used successfully.

When using psychological instruments, it is important to keep in mind their strengths and limitations. Psychological instruments should serve as only one part of an overall assessment. Professional judgment and additional data often are needed to evaluate whether results are valid for a particular individual. The publisher of a psychological instrument is required to set professional qualifications for its use and to restrict sales to persons who meet the qualifications. Publishers are also required to publish detailed test manuals providing information about item selection, normative samples, and research findings. Users should obtain and read these manuals carefully. The literature in this area, however, is sparse for persons with mental retardation. Studies using various instruments and procedures have limited reliability and validity because there is little consistency in the terminology and procedures across studies.

Much more research is needed on the epidemiology of mental health disorders in persons with mental retardation. At the present time, the best evidence suggests that overall prevalence rates tend to be higher for persons with mental retardation, primarily because of a greater vulnerability to environmental stressors. However, there is currently no convincing evidence that persons with mental retardation are especially vulnerable to psychotic, affective, or anxiety disorders when compared to persons who do not have mental retardation (Stark, Menolascino, Albarelli, and Gray, 1988). Service providers need to consider what is "normal" or "typical" behavior for any person in certain circumstances. For example, a death in the family may result in normal grieving by anyone, including persons with mental retardation. The latter simply may not be able to express it in the same way ways others do; but this expression does not make them mentally ill.

DIAGNOSTIC DIMENSIONS

The diagnosis of mental illness in persons with mental retardation requires the use of general diagnostic procedures, which can be divided into the following stages: (a) review of history, (b) comprehensive evaluation, (c) patient examination, (d) assessment, (e) diagnostic formulation, (f) intervention plans, (g) informing conference, and (h) follow-through (Szymanski, 1988). Because mental illness and mental retardation may coexist, the clinician must rely more on the signs (observed behaviors) and less on the symptoms (verbally reported distress of dysfunction) that characterize the various psychiatric disorders, especially in those individuals with more intense needs for supports. The principles of integrating multidisciplinary information into a comprehensive diagnostic process is recommended for different settings serving various degrees of these two conditions. As discussed earlier in this chapter, investigators have reported rather consistently a 20 to 35 percent frequency rate of mental illness in noninstitutionalized persons with mental retardation compared to 15 to 19 percent of the general population who meet the criteria of mental illness as defined by the American Psychiatric Association (Menolascino and Stark, 1984).

The most frequently reported types of mental illness in persons with mental retardation are:

- Schizophrenic Disorders
    Catatonic type
    Paranoid type
    Undifferentiated type
    Residual type
- Organic Brain Disorders
    Behavioral reaction
    Psychotic reaction
    Presenile dementia
- Adjustment Disorders
    Childhood and adolescent
    Disturbance of conduct
    Adulthood

- Personality Disorders
    Schizoid
    Paranoid
    Narcissistic
    Avoidant
    Passive-aggressive
    Antisocial
- Affective Disorders
    Unipolar manic disorders
    Bipolar affective
    Major depression recurrent
    Cyclothymic disorder

The following case studies illustrate some of the dynamics of mental illness in persons with mental retardation.

Case Study 1.* Miss A was a 23-year-old female with pervasive needs who had been living in a group home since the age of 19. The staff had noted a distinct behavioral change over the preceding 7 months, with decreased socialization and poor job performances at her structured workshop placement. They reported occasional episodes of giggling and stated that for the first time she had been observed talking and gesturing to herself. On several occasions, she awakened in the middle of the night, appearing very frightened. On examination, she appeared disheveled and distracted. She giggled for no apparent reason, often tilted her head for prolonged periods of time as if straining to hear something. Her answers to questions were frequently inappropriate and revealed a decrease from a previously documented higher level of functioning. Physical, radiologic, and metabolic examinations were unremarkable. Evaluation by a psychiatric consultant eventuated in a diagnosis of schizophreniform psychosis; hospitalization at a local psychiatric institute was recommended and accomplished. Treatment was initiated, utilizing a combination of milieu therapy, group psychotherapy, and antipsychotic medication. Over the next 3 weeks, there was a gradual reduction in inappropriate laughter and hallucinations and an improvement in spontaneous vocalization, sleep, and social contact with others. Her free-hand drawings had initially been marked by pictures of knives, bloody scenes, and religious themes; it was noted that she slowly began to produce the animal and flower themes that she had excelled at in the past. As she improved, she was slowly reintroduced into her work setting and did very well in that setting. She was discharged 6 weeks following admission and continued on a low dose of thiothixene for outpatient follow-up.

Case Study 2. Mr. B was a 52-year-old male with limited needed supports. He was committed to a psychiatric hospital by the police after an altercation surrounding his refusal to leave the house in which he had been living. The house belonged to his uncle, who allowed him to live there following the death of his mother 2 years previously. At that time, Mr. B had suffered a depressive episode that had been successfully treated with electroconvulsive therapy. His uncle had reported that he had told Mr. B that he wanted to sell the house 6 months before Mr. B was admitted to the hospital, but that Mr. B had refused to leave or cooperate with the uncle in making other living arrangements. During that time, he had been having daily crying spells and difficulty falling asleep, had increased his food intake and gained 30 pounds, had broken furniture, had cursed at visitors, and believed that his uncle was conspiring to put him in prison. On examination, he was moderately obese, and his speech was characterized by significant dysarthria. His responses to most questions were monosyllabic, and he repeatedly and angrily talked about "taking me to jail." Otherwise, his affect was flat and his mood appeared depressed. When asked about his feelings and his family, he quickly became tearful and would talk less. The physical examination and allied laboratory evaluations were within normal limits. The diagnosis of major depression disorder, recurrent, with psychotic features was made, and treatment was initiated with individual psychotherapy, group psychotherapy, and tricyclic antidepressant medication. He slowly responded and began to be able to talk about his home and family. By the third hospital week, his sleep had improved, his crying spells had disappeared, and he had no further delusions of persecution. He was discharged to a group home and workshop in his community and received outpatient psychiatric follow-up.

*These case histories are adapted from those presented in Menolascino and Stark (1984).

Case Study 3. Mr. C was a 19-year-old male with pervasive needed supports who had been residing in group homes most of his life. He had been in his current placement for the preceding 3 years and had done quite well there in a specialized work setting, until 2 months prior to his admission. At that time, two simultaneous events took place that were disruptive to him: Two of the caretakers at the group home setting left and were replaced within one week by two strangers; in addition, because of a medical problem, Mr. C's roommate was hospitalized, and Mr. C received a new roommate who was significantly older and displayed persistent behavioral problems. The new roommate would often remain awake throughout the night, pacing or playing his radio loudly, in spite of staff admonitions. Over the subsequent 2 months, there was a gradual change in Mr. C's behavior in that he, too, became sleepless at night and began roaming around within the group home or leaving it at night, necessitating that staff members follow him and return him to the home. At the same time, his performance in the specialized work setting deteriorated, and he became increasingly involved in minor verbal altercations with several of his co-workers and staff members there. He became more generally active and spent more time in seemingly purposeless motor activity; he was also noted to be somewhat irritable and would often engage in verbal baiting of some of his acquaintances in the community residence.

At the time of admission, he stubbornly discussed his current situation and noted that he was upset; he wondered what had happened to his roommate and to former friends and staff members. Initially, in the hospital, he had difficulty falling asleep, less than optimal appetite, and much purposeless motor behavior. He also seemed to be quite anxious and would spend extended periods of time muttering to himself. There were no apparent psychotic symptoms and no other symptoms of depression. Physical and laboratory examinations were unremarkable. He was treated with a combination of individual and group psychotherapy as well as a continued highly structured work program but with no medication. Within 10 days of his admission, most of his presenting symptoms had disappeared, and he began to be reintroduced into his community group-home placement. He seemed to do much better than prior to his admission. During this time, his original roommate had returned, and on discharge, he was able to resume his old relationship with his former roommate. Final diagnoses were adjustment disorder with mixed disturbance of emotions and conduct.

Case Study 4. Mr. D was a 35-year-old male with limited needed supports who was admitted to the psychiatric hospital for the second time. His history revealed a chaotic childhood involving termination of his parent's rights when he was 2 years old and multiple transfers between a series of foster homes and orphanage placements between the ages of 2 and 16. During this time, there had been numerous incidents of running away from various foster homes, arrests during runaways for drug abuse and shoplifting, some minor vandalism, poor school performance, and several physical altercations with peers and, on one occasion, with a police officer. His chaotic lifestyle had persisted, and he had been arrested twice for theft and had spent a brief time in a county jail following the theft of an automobile. He had continued to abuse drugs and alcohol and had gathered a reputation as a barroom brawler, especially when intoxicated. He had been married and divorced once and then had lived with and left a second partner after impregnating her. He maintained limited employment, usually working as a laborer, but on one occasion was involved as a helper in a local truck-driving operation for a period of 7 months. He had spent a great deal of his adult life, between his marriage and involvement with his second partner, living in missions, panhandling, and traveling around the country.

The current hospitalization had been precipitated by some out-of-contact behavior that had occurred during a period of intoxication, and he had been transferred by police officers from a local jail to the psychiatric hospital. The just related history had been obtained from the patient, who seemed to take a certain delight in recounting some of his past illegal or shady activities and from a family member who was willing to give a history but unwilling to have any other contact with the patient, "Because he has burned me too many times before." The diagnostic impression was antisocial personality disorder. He was singularly uninterested in treatment opportunities and, following his court appearance for the problems that had prompted his admission, he was discharged to an uncle in a distant state who felt that farm work would "straighten him out real quick." The prognosis for this gentleman was considered poor.

TREATMENT ISSUES

Despite inadequacies in our current information-gathering, the evidence from numerous studies indicates lessened habilitation outcomes for persons with mental retardation/ mental illnesses, such as (a) initial out-of-home placement, reinstitutionalization; (b) failure in the community placements and readmissions to supervised residential placements; (c) reduced employment prospects; and (d) reduced opportunity for social integration and leisure in community settings (Fletcher, 1988; Lewis and MacLean, 1982).

Thus, one of the greatest needs for persons with both mental retardation and some form of diagnosed mental illness is to implement habilitation programs that will enhance the person's independence/interdependence, productivity, and community integration. In addition to good habilitation services for persons with mental retardation, such habilitation programs frequently include both chemical and behavioral support paradigms. Suggested guidelines for these supports in habilitation programs are:

1. Possible alternative treatment interventions should be reviewed that could alter disturbing sets of behavior.

2. A specific plan should be formulated for each client, regardless of the setting.

3. The use of any psychoactive agent should be within an overall treatment approach.

4. The treatment coordinator should be requested to review and record the current effect of the prescribed medication.

5. Combination of psychoactive agents with duplicate pharmacodynamic effects should be avoided.

6. Combination of neuroleptic agents with antianxiety agents should be avoided.

7. Use of the psychoactive agents should be contained within established clinical practice limits.

8. Psychoactive medications should be used carefully with people who are young, elderly, and/or medically fragile.

9. All treatment staff members should be informed as to the side effects of the medications and the most common drug interactions.

10. An established drug review of each client should occur on a regular time interval.

PSYCHOPHARMACOLOGICAL SUPPORTS

Psychopharmacological agents have a profound effect on the cognitive and behavioral functions of persons with mental retardation and mental illness (Argan and Martin, 1985). For example, possible interactions of the anticonvulsant agents with other treatment modalities for persons with mental retardation should be assessed. It is important to maintain an individual's maximum cognitive ability while reaching the greatest efficacy of the psychopharmacological agents and the anticonvulsant medications (Hill, Balow, and Bruininks, 1985). Behavioral goals of psychopharmacological therapy are as follows:

- Reduction of Arousal Symptoms
  Psychomotor excitement
  Restlessness
  Irritability
  Aggressiveness
  Distractibility
  Insomnia
- Improvement in Affective Symptoms
  Flat affect
  Labile affect
  Somatic complaints
  Anxiety
  Anhedonia
  Inappropriate affect
  Social withdrawal
  Isolation
  Depression
- Improvement in Perceptual Functioning
  Hallucinations
  Illusions
- Improvement in Cognitive Processes
  Loose associations
  Flight of ideas
  Delusions

- Improvement in Verbal Communication
  Incoherence
  Echolalia
  Symbolism
  Neologisms
  Stereotypal language
  Mutism
- Improvement in Behavioral Symptoms
  Mannerisms
  Stereotypical behaviors
  Echopraxia
  Negativism
  Catalepsy
  Deteriorated manners
- Improvement in the Features of Attention Deficit Disorder with Hyperactivity
  Excessive motor activity
  Attention difficulties
  Inability to sit still
  Poorly organized activity
  Impulsivity
  Disruption of others
  Variable behavior

Although the results of psychopharmacological supports are equivocal, some conclusions can be made from drug studies involving people with mental retardation. The most important of these include:

1. Psychopharmacologic intervention can be very effective in reducing specific target symptoms and achieving a more integrated level of cognitive functioning.

2. Psychopharmacologic intervention is most effective when combined with a transdisciplinary treatment and management approach.

3. The level of therapeutic response of a psychoactive drug appears to have little effect on actual cognitive level of functioning.

4. Extremely high or prolonged use of neuroleptic medication tends to cause a reduction in learning, cognition, and performance as well as increasing the risk of tardive dyskinesia.

5. Growth in children does not appear to be significantly affected if used intermittently or at lower doses.

6. There is a lack of clinical studies involving the use of psychoactive drugs other than neuroleptics.

7. Serious methodological problems have been noted in many drug studies, namely, the lack of placebo controls, nonspecification or misuse of random assignment, inappropriate statistics or no statistical analysis, unknown reliability of rating scales, and vague reporting techniques.

BEHAVIORAL SUPPORTS

There is a growing body of literature suggesting that many persons who have mental retardation/mental illness can function very well (and indeed better in many cases) with less psychotropic medication (Gualtieri, 1988). This finding, combined with the current "technology of behavior support" indicates that, consistent with the definition in this manual, the intensities and type of supports provided to these persons is critical in diagnostic and classification efforts. Specifically, Table 5.2 summarizes a number of nonaversive, behavioral support functions that should form the basis for habilitation services to these persons.

In this chapter we have stressed a number of considerations for persons potentially diagnosed as having mental retardation/mental illness. Although these individuals have frequently and historically been denied high quality services because of the complexity of their behaviors, their future can be quite different. With a renewed commitment to environmental and behavioral systems of supports, and the judicious use of medication, this group of people can experience increased independence, productivity, and community integration.

TABLE 5.2   Basic Principles of the Technology of Behavioral Support

1. Instruction Control
- Physically arrange the environment
- Keep active and interactive with others
- Use errorless learning (task analysis, assistance, encouragement)
- Fade assistance as soon as possible

2. Functional Analysis (Antecedent–Behavior–Consequence)

3. Multicomponent Interventions
- Natural environment
- Ignore–redirect–reward
- Multiple opportunities for choice-making
- Staff training

4. Importance of Ecological and Setting Events
- Medication
- Nutrition
- Stress management
- Exercise
- Sleeping patterns

5. Teaching of Social Skills

6. Building of Environments With Effective Consequences

7. Minimizing Use of Punishment

8. Distinguishing Emergency Procedures From Proactive Programming

CHAPTER 6

DIMENSION III: HEALTH AND PHYSICAL CONSIDERATIONS

IMPORTANCE OF HEALTH

Health is a fundamental aspect of living and includes several important personal capabilities, such as strength, vitality, alertness, and sensorimotor abilities. Although these personal capabilities are not among those necessarily affected in the model of mental retardation described in chapter 2, health and physical functioning are often relevant because of their effects on the model and its components. In this chapter these effects and the relation of health to the identification and classification of people with mental retardation are described.

For people with mental retardation, the effects of health on functioning also influence assessment, environmental factors, and the need for supports and services. The importance of health is reflected by its place on Dimension III of the Definition, Classification, and Systems of Supports. In this chapter we first describe these effects on functioning, assessment, and needed supports. The complexity of health-related concerns and key issues in the diagnosis of health problems are then described. This approach should facilitate accurate description of health and physical functioning and coding of any existing health problems on Dimension III. Needed supports are identified and the implications for research on health and physical functioning are discussed.

IMPACT ON FUNCTIONING

For people with mental retardation, the effects of health on functioning range from greatly facilitating to greatly inhibiting. An example of vigorous good health with excellent physical abilities might be a young athlete with mental retardation who is victorious in Special Olympics competition. Some athletes with mental retardation might be able to compete successfully in school sports and extracurricular activities with their age peers who are not affected by mental retardation, and these individuals should have the opportunity to choose to participate. For them, the impact of good health on functioning is facilitative. Any limitation in opportunities is likely related to discrimination rather than health problems.

On the other hand, an example of severely impaired health that greatly inhibits functioning would be a person with mental retardation who is also affected by severe cerebral palsy and epilepsy. This individual might be nonambulatory; virtually immobile with little or no spontaneous movement; unable to chew or swallow, and, thus, dependent on a gastrostomy tube for nutrition and hydration; and required to take a number of medications to control seizures. People so severely affected physically are also susceptible to other health problems, such as recurrent infections (pneumonia, sepsis), nutritional deficiencies (reduced absorption of calories, vitamins, minerals), and orthopedic disorders (fractures, dislocation, contractures, scoliosis). Indeed, the magnitude of these effects on physical functioning is such that life expectancy may be greatly shortened (Eyman, Grossman, Chaney, and Call, 1990).

The great majority of people with mental retardation function somewhere between these extremes. They may have some difficulty with mobility, including impairments in strength, tone, coordination, or movement. They may have some difficulty with vision or hearing. They may have a variety of other health problems, such as obesity, hypertension, scoliosis, chronic ear infection, or seizures (McDonald, 1985; Rubin, 1987; Rubin and Crocker, 1989). These health problems are not inherently different from those of people who do not have mental retardation. The effects of these problems may, however, be different because of environments, coping limitations, and impediments in health care systems.

If there is a different effect on functioning for people with mental retardation, it may be partly because of the environments in which they live, learn, work, play, socialize, and interact with others. Their environments may create unique dangers or fail to provide appropriate protection and treatment (Conroy, 1985). In addition, the intellectual limitations of people with mental retardation may make it more difficult for them to cope with these associated physical problems. These coping problems may be manifested as difficulty in negotiating the health services system, poor understanding of treatment needs, difficulty with communication, and use of alternative and misinterpreted symptoms, such as self-injurious behavior. They may need individually designed health training to address these and other issues. The structure of health services delivery systems may impede access to health care, so these individuals may need training and assistance in negotiating these systems. Actual physical functioning of people with mental retardation is influenced by the existence of health problems (impairments in physical capabilities), by the nature of the person's living environment, and by the effects of intellectual and adaptive limitations on coping with physical disorders. All of these influences on functioning have important implications for assessment and supports.

IMPACT ON ASSESSMENT

Chapter 4 emphasizes that professionals must utilize a valid instrument that is not unduly influenced by coexisting physical impairments. For example, tests that depend on verbal abilities would fail to measure adequately the intelligence of a person with severe cerebral palsy who is unable to speak. Similarly, special tests of intelligence are necessary in the presence of significant sensory disorders, such as impaired vision or hearing problems.

The impact of impaired alertness and vitality may be particularly important during assessment. Alertness may be reduced if an individual has sleep disturbances, chronic illness, or is taking certain medications, such as anticonvulsants or tranquilizers. Even such commonly used drugs as phenobarbital may cause reduced performance on tests of intelligence (Farwell et al., 1990). A common early effect of malnutrition on vitality may be manifested as apathy and disinterest (Davis, 1988) and may cause people with mental retardation who are malnourished to perform below their actual capability level on intelligence tests. Tiredness and fatigue may also affect test performance for individuals with coexisting chronic illnesses, such as those accompanied by chronic hypoxia or congestive heart failure.

The assessment of adaptive skills may also be affected by health problems. Many of the influences of health problems on the assessment of intelligence just noted also apply for adaptive skills. Therapeutic drugs may affect adaptive skills and influence assessment. For example, the anticonvulsant drug phenytoin may impair coordination and motor skills, particularly when serum drug levels are high (Dodrill and Troupin, 1991). During the assessment of adaptive skills, it may be difficult to separate the influences of health problems that may interfere with valid measurement of the skill area from influences of health problems on the skill area itself. For example, assessment of communication skills may be affected by the presence of an oral motor disorder. Provision of augmentative or alternative communication technology could allow such individuals to compensate for this physical problem and thereby demonstrate their actual communication skills. In this example, valid assessment of this adaptive skill is dependent on the availability and provision of appropriate supports that permit optimal functioning.

NEED FOR SUPPORTS

The process of determining the need for appropriate supports is described in chapter 9, and the application of this process to health is described later in this chapter. The present section contains descriptions of areas in which supports may be needed because of the impact of health on functioning, for example, making available opportunities for community inclusion, providing access to health services, and ensuring a safe environment.

Individuals with mental retardation who have physical limitations may have reduced opportunities for participation in the life of their community primarily because of these limitations. For example, if seizures are not well-controlled, a person may be forced to live in a more restricted and supervised environment in order to maintain safeguards against seizure-related injuries. If a person has impaired mobility and cannot walk independently, community participation may be limited by lack of wheelchair access and appropriate transportation services. If a person has significantly impaired vision or hearing, vocational opportunities for supported or independent work in the community may be restricted because of limited availability of appropriate jobs. In each of these examples, provision of adequate supports could increase inclusion of the individual in the life of the community.

Access to health services is often a limiting factor for people with mental retardation. All individuals need primary health care services, such as routine examinations, screening and prevention programs, and immunizations. In addition, most persons need acute health care services from time to time because of occasional illnesses or injuries. Those who have chronic health problems need ongoing long-term health care services from a consistent provider. Access to any or all of these services may be limited because of inadequate health care financing, for example, if the person with mental retardation is inadequately insured or is covered by public insurance programs that are not accepted by all health care providers (Howard, 1991). Even when adequate insurance coverage is present, some providers may be reluctant to accept people with mental retardation because of the provider's lack of training or discomfort when treating them (Garrard, 1982). Health services utilization also may be limited because many individuals with mental retardation do not receive individualized training in personal health care. Lack of access to quality health care services increases the likelihood that the individual with mental retardation will receive inadequate health care, which would likely result in impaired functioning. Provision of sufficient supports to assure access to quality health care services would ensure optimal functioning through treatment of whatever health problems may exist or develop.

Ensuring a safe environment is necessary for all people with mental retardation whose ability to recognize and respond to danger is limited. Many people incorrectly assume that this is easier to accomplish in restricted environments than in the community at large (Stark, Menolascino, Albarelli, and Gray, 1988). Thus, the need for a safe environment can limit the extent to which a person with mental retardation is able to participate in community activities. As a general principle, the level of risk inherent in the environment of individuals with mental retardation should be no greater than the level of risk in the general community. Appropriate supports, such as personal safety training, safe and available transportation, supervision during community activities when indicated, protection in group living arrangements, criminal records checks on service providers, and improved criminal laws and prosecution of abusers, can reduce these environmental risks without restricting community inclusion. Supports that enhance safety reduce the likelihood of injury, promote good health, and facilitate optimal functioning within the community.

COMPLEXITY OF HEALTH CONCERNS

People with mental retardation may have health problems that require special attention because of their complexity. For some individuals, the underlying disorder that is the etiology of the mental retardation may also predispose the individual to other health problems. Certain genetic disorders, such as Down syndrome or tuberous sclerosis, can affect the heart, kidneys, or spine. Other disorders, such as spina bifida, also can affect multiple organ systems. The complexity of the health services needs of individuals with these health problems requires a coordinated and often multidisciplinary approach by a team of health professionals (Ziring, Kastner, and Friedman, 1988).

Many individuals with mental retardation who have complex health care needs will function well when these requirements are met appropriately. Others will still have severely limited functioning because of the magnitude of their associated health problems. The term *medical fragility* is sometimes used to indicate how vulnerable such individuals are to seemingly slight changes that can greatly compromise their health status. For example, a person with mental retardation who is nonambulatory, has limited mobility, is unable to swallow food by mouth, and has chronic lung disease (from the effects of prematurity, chronic aspiration, or severe scoliosis) is vulnerable to malnutrition, metabolic disturbances, and overwhelming infections. The effect on health status of any or all of these complications can be quite severe and may even be life-threatening. As noted previously, such individuals have a markedly shortened life expectancy because of their vulnerability to these complications (Eyman et al., 1990). The intensity of health services required by these individuals reflects the complexity of their health problems.

Furthermore, managing the complexity of these problems requires a variety of often highly specialized supports and services that must be integrated by health providers to assure a coordinated service plan.

At the other extreme, some individuals may function well enough that they are not recognized by health service providers as having mental retardation. Indeed, many individuals may seek to mask their disability and to "pass" as not having disabilities. This may be advantageous in terms of inclusion but also may create unique problems. Without special attention to the cognitive capabilities of the individual with mental retardation, the health care visit may be severely compromised. The provider may assume that the individual is able to describe his or her symptoms adequately and, thus, may neglect to inquire specifically about symptoms that the individual did not recognize as important, which could result in an incomplete or erroneous diagnosis. The provider may also assume that the individual understands the treatment plan and is capable of following it. If the provider does not take special care to explain the treatment plan in terms the individual can understand, adherence may be limited and the treatment may not be effective. The provider may wrongly assume the individual has given valid consent for diagnostic procedures or treatment when in fact the elements of consent are not completely present (H. Turnbull, 1977). These problems are more likely to occur when the provider has little or no experience with individuals who have mental retardation. This underscores the need for better training of health care providers.

DIAGNOSTIC ISSUES

Some of the problems involved in making a diagnosis of a health problem in individuals with mental retardation have already been mentioned. These and other diagnostic problems are summarized in the following discussion.

RECOGNIZING SYMPTOMS

The first step in obtaining health care is recognizing that a particular feeling or condition is unusual and might represent a significant problem. For example, an occasional headache may be attributed to stress and not interpreted as a significant health problem, but frequent or unexplainable headaches may be more worrisome and warrant investigation by a health care provider. The point at which these feelings or conditions become recognized as symptoms that warrant attention is the entry point into the health services delivery system. People with mental retardation may have difficulty determining that these feelings or conditions are unusual and could reflect a health problem, and, thus, they may fail to seek attention for them.

DESCRIBING SYMPTOMS

Once attention is sought from a health care provider, a person with mental retardation may have difficulty describing the symptom or condition adequately for the purpose of diagnosis. If the person is nonverbal, his or her feelings may have to be inferred from behavioral cues by those who know the person well. A sore throat may be expressed as loss of appetite, or stomach irritation may be expressed as a change in food preference favoring bland, neutral foods or milk products. Headache pain may be expressed as self-injurious behavior, such as head-banging or hitting, and other types of pain may be expressed as random, aggressive behavior. Even if the person is verbal, the description of the symptom may be too limited for precise diagnosis. If asked about the quality, intensity, or reactivity of the pain, the person may simply reply that it hurts. Some aspects of this process of inferring and understanding symptoms are similar to those used with children, but health care providers cannot rely on this analogy when treating adults with mental retardation. For example, the symptom may be one that children do not often have, such as angina or gallstones.

PHYSICAL EXAMINATION

Much of the physical examination depends on obtaining the person's cooperation. Without training or adequate preparation, a person with mental retardation may resist the examination or have difficulty understanding and responding appropriately to the examiner's request. Some individuals may not be able to cooperate when asked to take a deep breath, for example, or may be unable to respond appropriately when asked, "Does it hurt here?" when the examiner presses on a certain area. Thus, the ability to obtain detailed diagnostic information from the physical examination may be limited because typical examination procedures are not possible.

MULTIPLE PROBLEMS

Interpreting symptoms and physical findings may be difficult because of the presence of multiple health problems. For example, constipation may be caused by reduced fluid intake, a diet low in bulk because of difficulty chewing and swallowing, reduced general mobility because of cerebral palsy, an intestinal disorder, a side-effect of medication prescribed for some other health problem, or a combination of these factors. Diagnosing the actual cause of the symptom being evaluated requires knowledge of the effects and interactions of whatever other health problems may exist and the treatments that have been provided for them.

PREEXISTING DISORDERS

Many individuals with mental retardation may have preexisting health problems that may or may not be associated to the symptoms being evaluated. These preexisting disorders may be related to the etiology of the mental retardation as previously noted. For example, rapid breathing due to pneumonia may be difficult to recognize as an acute change if the person has a history of chronic lung disease resulting from prematurity. Changes in certain laboratory tests due to acute health problems may be difficult to recognize if the test results are abnormal due to a preexisting disorder, or the chronically abnormal test result may be misinterpreted as indicative of an acute disorder. Appropriate use of laboratory tests in such situations requires careful distinction between the effects of preexisting disorders and the effects of whatever new health problem may be present.

MAKING A DIAGNOSIS

Once the considerations just noted have been taken into account, the health care provider should make the most accurate diagnosis possible. In some situations, more than one diagnosis will be necessary to represent and describe the person's health status completely. For example, the provider may diagnose congestive heart failure due to excessive fluid intake in a person with congenital heart disease caused by Down syndrome. Each diagnosis should be listed separately in Dimension III of the Definition, Classifications, and Systems of Supports for individuals with mental retardation.

For coding purposes, the standard codes for each diagnosis listed in nationally recognized systems, such as the International Classification of Diseases (ICD) or Current Procedural Terminology (CPT), can be added.

GOOD HEALTH

If no health problems exist, this should be indicated on Dimension III (See Figure 3.3.). If the person has particular strengths in the area of health or physical functioning, such as athletic abilities or robust fitness, this should also be noted. Because these are not diagnoses of disease states or health problems, coding will not be possible and a narrative description may be most appropriate.

CRITICAL NEEDED SUPPORTS

Supports for health can be conceptualized in accordance with the generic model of supports and outcomes shown in Figure 9.1. In this model, the three aspects of support—resources, functions, and intensities—jointly influence the desired outcomes.

HEALTH RESOURCES

All individuals with mental retardation have personal resources that affect health. Genetic background can have a positive influence, for example, a family history of longevity or no family history of cancer or heart disease. Genetic influences can also predispose to health problems, either because of family tendencies to specific problems or because of the etiology of the individual's mental retardation. For example, Down syndrome may be associated with heart disease as well as mental retardation. Personal health resources also include health behaviors that may predispose the person to health problems or prevent them. Careful attention to nutrition, weight control, exercise, posture and balance, sleep habits, and personal stress management can prevent health problems. Adherence to safer sexual activity and avoidance of alcohol, tobacco, and drugs are as important for people with mental retardation as for anyone else.

Other people can be a health resource for individuals with mental retardation, for example, the person who accompanies the individual with mental retardation to health care visits. This person often has the primary responsibility for describing the symptoms to the provider and for adherence with the treatment plan. The outcome of the visit may depend in large part on how well this person interprets the symptoms to the provider and how capable he or she is of explaining the provider's advice and instructions to the individual with mental retardation and/or others in the home, school, or work site. Others who may be health resources include the network of health care providers—physicians, nurses, therapists, nutritionists, and counselors.

Technical resources for health include all of the forms of prescriptive assistance, such as medications; ventilatory assists; physical, occupational, and speech therapies; and orthotic devices, such as seating and braces. They also include assistive devices that facilitate functioning, such as those that improve mobility, communication, or self-help skills, to the extent that improved functioning promotes healthy behavior. For example, mobility assistance can facilitate exercise, or gastrostomy feeding can promote improved nutrition.

SUPPORT FUNCTIONS

Support functions include training in the development of good health behaviors and in the use of health resources as described previously as well as assisting in the achievement of these behaviors and in accessing and utilizing available personal, social, and technical resources, such as those already described. Mentoring is an important support function for health when it provides guidance, leadership, and role modeling of healthy behavior. Transportation is a support function for health to the extent that it facilitates accessing health care services, assisting the individual during the health care visit and adhering to the treatment plan.

INTENSITIES OF SUPPORTS

Habilitation goals related to health include promotion of healthy behavior, prevention of illness, treatment of disease, and amelioration of health-related disability. According to the Support Planning Matrix described in chapter 9 (see Table 9.2), individuals with mental retardation may require more or less support in achieving these health-related habilitation goals. The types of supports required are primarily provision of the previously described resources, coordination of health services, and assurance of quality in the services received. The family provides these supports for many individuals with mental retardation but may need considerable assistance. Appropriate supports for the family may be financial, logistical, social, or therapeutic in nature. Virtually all individuals with mental retardation will require some support for achievement of health-related goals. Limited support might consist of the availability of adequate health insurance through the work site or access to exercise and health promotion programs in the community. Extensive and pervasive intensities of supports include provision of some or all of the resources described in this chapter. Access to health care services in the community (including availability of adequate health care financing and generic providers whenever appropriate) is a critically important component of this support. Provision of whatever intensities of supports are needed will facilitate achievement of the desired outcomes, namely, maximizing opportunities for fulfillment of those habilitation goals related to health.

RESEARCH IMPLICATIONS

The need for more research on the health of people with mental retardation was emphasized by Garrard (1982) and has been re-emphasized by many others since that time. Research into the basic mechanisms of all diseases must include those conditions associated with mental retardation. The etiology and epidemiology of mental retardation should be investigated in order to facilitate more effective prevention programs. Researchers on the health care needs of people with mental retardation must focus on the full range of health-related variables existing in all settings. All aspects of health and illness need to be examined in relation to individuals with mental retardation (as they are for other people) in order to develop improved systems for providing them with health services delivery. A particularly acute need exists for research on the health status of people with mental retardation living in the community. The relations among health care needs, provision of resources, and achievement of desired outcomes related to health should be examined. Indeed, virtually every aspect of health and physical functioning of people with mental retardation is in need of much more research of much better quality. Conducting this research and bringing it to fruition are important challenges now and in the future.

CHAPTER 7

DIMENSION III: ETIOLOGY CONSIDERATIONS

Consideration of the etiology of mental retardation is an important aspect of classification for several reasons:

1. The etiology may be associated with other health-related problems that influence physical functioning as described in Dimension III of the Definition, Classification, and Systems of Supports.

2. The etiology may be treatable: Accurate early diagnosis of the etiology may permit appropriate treatment and prevent or minimize mental retardation.

3. Epidemiologic information derived from classification of persons with mental retardation is necessary for the design and evaluation of programs to prevent specific etiologies of mental retardation (Rowitz, 1984).

4. Comparison of individuals with mental retardation for certain research or administrative purposes or for some aspects of clinical practice depends on the formation of maximally homogeneous groups composed of individuals with the same or similar etiologies recorded on Dimension III.

In this chapter current thinking about the etiology of mental retardation is reviewed, and the complex, multifactorial, and often intergenerational nature of these etiologic considerations are emphasized. This current knowledge replaces the single-factor approach that was implied or stated explicitly in previous editions of the manual. This new knowledge is relevant because it requires a more comprehensive understanding of the many factors that may cause or contribute to mental retardation. Assigning an etiology cannot be reduced to picking a diagnosis from a long list of possibilities. These new concepts about etiology are also relevant because they are linked closely with efforts to prevent mental retardation. One cannot prevent what one does not understand. A multifactorial and intergenerational approach can also be applied to the design and evaluation of prevention programs.

Current knowledge permits development of a clinical framework for understanding etiology that can be applied to the classification of persons with mental retardation. In this chapter a clinical approach to the evaluation, assessment, assignment, and coding of the etiology of mental retardation is described. An outline of most presently identified etiologies is included. Using this approach to identify etiology on Dimension III will facilitate achievement of the purposes just described. We must stress that precise classification is highly desirable in the area of etiology and prevention for the reasons just given. This precision may be greater than that recommended or possible in other areas of the Definition, Classification, and Systems of Supports because a comparable degree of precision would not serve the purposes of classification in those other areas. In a functional classification such as this one, the degree of precision used should be justifiable in terms of the practical utility of the data.

Designation of the etiology is complicated by the fact that present knowledge is insufficient to identify the etiology of many persons with mental retardation. A recent review of 13 epidemiological studies concluded that for approximately 30 percent of cases identified as severe mental retardation and approximately 50 percent of cases identified as mild mental retardation, the cause is unknown (McLaren and Bryson, 1987). Masland (1988) pointed out, however, that just because the cause is not known does not mean that a cause does not exist, and continuing effort is needed to understand the etiology of those cases now classified as unknown. It is possible that the cause in at least some of these cases is related to developmental disturbances in neuronal connectivity mediated by dendritic, axonal, synaptic, or glial mechanisms, a concept that has been termed *hypoconnection* to indicate the potential neurobiological origin of inefficient information processing (Coulter, 1987). The precise etiology of these disturbances in connectivity remains to be elucidated through better understanding of the genetic and environmental processes that contribute to brain development. Some of these genetic processes only affect brain development before birth and, thus, may be difficult to detect after birth (Huttenlocher, 1991). Molecular genetic research on fetal brain development will likely help to elucidate these mechanisms that may be responsible for the etiology in many cases that are currently classified as unknown. Adverse environmental influences on brain development before and after birth include malnutrition and the effects of toxins, such as alcohol or lead (Kavanagh, 1988; Menolascino and Stark, 1988; Pueschel and Mulick, 1990). In addition, the adverse influence of environmental deprivation on mental development may be related to developmental alterations of neural connectivity during critical periods of brain development (Coulter, 1987). Greater precision in identifying and understanding these adverse environmental influences will likely clarify the etiology of many cases of mental retardation currently classified as unknown.

MULTIFACTORIAL ASPECTS OF ETIOLOGY

The etiology of mental retardation has historically been divided into two broad categories or typologies: mental retardation of biological origin and mental retardation due to psychosocial disadvantage. This distinction no longer stands, however. McLaren and Bryson (1987) noted in their review of epidemiological studies of mental retardation that as much as 50 percent of the population of persons with mental retardation have more than one possible causal factor. Furthermore, mental retardation often reflects the cumulative or interactive effects of more than one factor. Similarly, Scott (1988) observed that from a public health perspective, the data do not support separating the etiology of mental retardation into biological and psychosocial categories. He proposed a multiple-risk-factor approach, which would include factors from both categories that may interact to cause mental retardation. As an example, low birth weight is often considered to be a "biological" etiology, but the antecedents of low birth weight may be "psychosocial" factors such as maternal youth, poverty, lack of education, and inadequate prenatal care. Thus, the historical distinction between biological and psychosocial types may be blurred in many cases (Rowitz, 1986). The observations that multiple risk factors converge to predispose an individual to the disabling process and that risk factors interact at different stages of the disabling process are central to current thinking about disability (Institute of Medicine, 1991).

A multifactorial approach to etiology requires expansion of the list of causal factors in two directions: types of factors and timing of factors. One direction extends the types or categories of etiologic factors into four groupings:

1. *Biomedical*: factors that relate to biologic processes, such as genetic disorders or nutrition

2. *Social*: factors that relate to social and family interaction, such as stimulation and adult responsiveness

3. *Behavioral*: factors that relate to potentially causal behaviors, such as dangerous (injurious) activities or maternal substance abuse

4. *Educational*: factors that relate to the availability of educational supports that promote mental development and the development of adaptive skills

The second direction describes the timing of the occurrence of causal factors according to whether these factors affect the parents of the person with mental retardation, the person with mental retardation, or both. This aspect of causality is termed *intergenerational* to describe the influence of factors present during one generation on the outcome in the next generation. Galler (1988) showed that animals who were malnourished during infancy, but later nourished adequately, had offspring that performed poorly on tests of learning and behavior. Ramey (1990) reported that human infants born to mothers with mental retardation had lower developmental scores at 3 years of age, but this decline could be prevented by comprehensive early intervention. This modern concept of intergenerational effects is different from and must not be confused with the historical pseudogenetic concept that is now widely repudiated. The old idea that mental retardation due to "psychosocial, cultural, or familial factors" was caused by "weak genes" in the family led to the widespread effort to remove such persons from society and to prevent their reproduction (Scheerenberger, 1983; J. Smith, 1985, 1989). This misguided attempt to prevent mental retardation failed to recognize that reversible environmental factors in the lives of these families were often responsible for mental retardation in those affected, and it denied persons with mental retardation the benefits of community inclusion and other interventions that would have improved their level of functioning. Current ideas about intergenerational effects stress their origin in preventable and reversible influences of adverse environments, and understanding these effects will facilitate community inclusion and enhance functioning.

These concepts concerning the multifactorial and intergenerational origins of mental retardation have important implications for prevention, which can be divided into three levels (Rowitz, 1986):

1. *Primary prevention* refers to actions that occur before the onset of the problem and that stop the problem from occurring (such as programs that prevent maternal alcohol abuse).

2. *Secondary prevention* refers to actions that shorten the duration of or reverse the effects of ("cure") existing problems (such as dietary programs to treat persons born with phenylketonuria).

3. *Tertiary prevention* refers to actions that limit the adverse consequences of a problem and improve the individual's level of functioning (such as programs for physical, educational, or vocational habilitation).

These concepts of prevention can be incorporated into an intergenerational model of the etiologies of mental retardation. Primary prevention efforts are directed toward the parents of the person with mental retardation or the person who might otherwise develop a condition that would result in mental retardation. Secondary prevention efforts are directed toward the person who is born with a condition that might otherwise result in mental retardation. Tertiary prevention efforts are directed toward the person who has mental retardation. Within each level of prevention, actions can be taken that affect each of the four groups of etiologic factors (biomedical, social, behavioral, and educational) previously mentioned. Some examples of specific programs for prevention of mental retardation are shown in Table 7.1 according to the etiologic factor, level of prevention, and generation affected. This table underscores the importance of an interactive and multifactorial approach to understanding the etiology of mental retardation and the importance of this approach to etiology for the design of programs to prevent mental retardation (Coulter, 1991b).

CLINICAL EVALUATION FOR ETIOLOGY

It is important to distinguish between the existence of an etiology commonly associated with mental retardation and the occurrence of pathophysiological mechanisms induced by that etiology. These mechanisms may or may not result in a level of performance within the range of mental retardation. Etiology is not destiny: An individual may have a condition that is considered to be an etiology of mental retardation, yet that individual's level of performance may not be in the range of mental retardation. Indeed, this possibility is the cornerstone of programs for secondary prevention as just described. Many individuals who have one of the conditions listed in Table 7.3, which appears at the end of this chapter, do not have mental retardation. The reason why a particular condition is included in this table is that at least some individuals with the condition do have mental retardation. Thus, for those individuals, the existence of the condition may be relevant to the etiology of their mental retardation.

This discussion of evaluation for etiology assumes that the individual has already been determined to have mental retardation according to the definition described in this manual and that mental retardation has been diagnosed on Dimension I of the Definition, Classification, and Systems of Supports. Therefore, this discussion does not include evaluation to determine the presence of mental retardation (see chapter 4). Rather, the purpose of this evaluation for etiology is to identify all of the causal factors that may be operative so that these factors may be listed on Dimension III of the Definition, Classification, and Systems of Supports.

TABLE 7.1   Etiology and Prevention of Mental Retardation: A Multidimensional Model

Type of prevention/ Recipient of service	Etiology factor			
	Biomedical	Social	Behavioral	Educational
Primary prevention *Parent[a]*				
Child	Lead screening Nutrition	Prevention of abuse/neglect	Acceptance	Sexuality
Teenager	Nutrition	Family support	Avoidance of substance use (or treatment)	Parenting
Parent to be	Prenatal care and screening Nutrition	Emotional and social support	Avoidance of substance use (or treatment)	Parenting
Primary and secondary prevention *Person with (or at risk for) mental retardation as:*				
Newborn	Metabolic screening	Parent/child interaction	– –	– –
Child	Nutrition Lead screening	Family support Avoidance of abuse/neglect	Avoidance of accidents and injuries	Early infant intervention Head Start Special education Vocational training
Tertiary prevention *Person with mental retardation as:*				
Adult	Health care	Inclusion	Independence	Productivity

[a] Parent of person with mental retardation at different stages of life.

MEDICAL HISTORY

The medical history begins at conception and can be divided into prenatal, perinatal, and postnatal phases. Information needed about the *prenatal period* includes maternal age; parity and health (including any maternal infections); the adequacy of maternal nutrition; the amount and quality of prenatal care (including prenatal screening or amniocentesis for potential problems); maternal use of drugs, alcohol, or other substances; maternal exposure to potential toxins or teratogens (such as lead or radiation); and occurrence of any significant maternal injuries or hyperthermia. Information needed about the *perinatal period* includes the occurrence of intrauterine disorders during labor and delivery, abnormalities of the process of labor and delivery, gestational age at birth, growth status at birth (including the presence of intrauterine growth retardation), Apgar scores at birth, and the occurrence of any neonatal disorders (such as hypoxicischemic encephalopathy, seizures, respiratory distress, infections, or metabolic disorders). Information needed about the *postnatal period* includes the occurrence of significant head injuries, infections, seizures, toxic and metabolic disorders (such as lead poisoning), significant malnutrition or impaired growth, and developmental regression possibly due to degenerative disorders (such as Tay-Sachs disease).

The medical history also includes a detailed family history of health status, medical illnesses, and mental functioning. Maternal or paternal relatives affected by conditions that may be associated with mental retardation, or who themselves were diagnosed with mental retardation, should be noted. The occurrence of mental retardation in the family, however, does not necessarily imply a genetic mechanism (for example, a relative may have mental retardation due to childhood meningitis or head injury).

PSYCHOSOCIAL EVALUATION

Information about the psychosocial environment is needed to evaluate possible social, behavioral, and educational factors that may have caused or contributed to the occurrence of mental retardation. Psychosocial information may be important for other aspects of classification as well, but it is considered here only in terms of the possible contribution of psychosocial factors to the etiology of mental retardation. The psychosocial environment may be considered in an ecological perspective by describing the characteristics of the individual, family, school or work setting, and community and cultural milieu (Bronfenbrenner, 1979). The reciprocal interactions among these elements of the environment may be considered by adopting a transactional view of development (Sameroff, 1986). Understanding the nature of these transactions between ecological subsystems of the psychosocial environment will assist in evaluation of their etiological impact on the functioning of the person with mental retardation.

When the intergenerational perspective is used, information is needed about the parents' social, educational, and psychological history. Information is also required about the structure, stability, and functioning of the immediate and extended family of the person with mental retardation. The developmental history of the individual with mental retardation includes a history of previous experiences, a history of any educational or therapeutic interventions, and a consideration of any associated mental disorders. The sociocultural milieu in which the individual develops is important because it may influence the psychosocial environment, including the local community, the country of origin, and specific ethnic, cultural, or religious factors that may affect environmental experiences and transactions.

Evaluation of the psychosocial environment may not yield any relevant information about causal factors in a particular case. Even when the etiology appears straightforward, however, psychosocial factors may prove to be contributory. For example, "obvious" etiologies, such as fetal alcohol syndrome, low birth weight, or childhood head injury, may be associated with significant social or behavioral factors that contributed to their occurrence. These factors should be included in a complete description of the etiology of mental retardation in such cases.

PHYSICAL EXAMINATION

The physical examination serves several distinct purposes. The usual purpose is to assist in the diagnosis of a medical problem, such as pneumonia or hypothyroidism, for which the individual has sought attention and that may warrant specific treatment. These aspects of diagnosis are considered in chapter 6 on health and physical considerations. The purpose considered in the present chapter is to assist in the identification of the etiology of mental retardation. A single physical examination may serve both purposes, but the conceptual distinction between them needs to be retained.

The physical examination may provide evidence of an obvious etiology often associated with mental retardation, such as Down syndrome. More often, however, it will provide only supportive evidence for an etiology suspected from other data (such as spastic diplegia associated with a history of premature birth), or it will not provide any useful information about etiology at all. For most individuals whose etiology is classified as unknown, the physical examination will be normal or noncontributory. Thus, one cannot expect the physical examination to answer every question about etiology. It is necessary, but it is only one component in the clinical evaluation for etiology and in many cases may not be the most important component.

Information needed from the physical examination includes anthropometric measurements of growth (height, weight, and head circumference), which should be plotted against age on graphs that are appropriate for the individual's status. Additional physical measurements may be contributory (Jones, 1988). Detailed examination of the head, eyes, ears, nose, throat, glands, heart, blood vessels, lungs, abdomen, genitalia, spine, extremities, and skin should be conducted. Any major or minor malformations should be noted (Aase, 1990; Feingold and Pashayan, 1983; Jones, 1988). A detailed neurologic examination should include evaluation for any focal or generalized deficits (DeJong, 1979; Paine and Oppe, 1966). Specific neurologic findings will rarely indicate the etiology by themselves, but some findings (such as nystagmus, hypotonia, or ataxia) may be important clues to the actual etiology.

ASSESSMENT OF ETIOLOGIC INFORMATION

The information derived from the clinical evaluation needs to be examined and assessed because some data may be more relevant to the etiology of mental retardation than are other data. Furthermore, the available data may be sufficient only to provide clues or ideas that warrant further investigation. When the etiology is not obvious from the clinical evaluation, it is often helpful to list the most likely possibilities. This list, which is often referred to as the differential diagnosis of the problem, can be considered as a series of hypotheses regarding possible etiologies. For example, the clinical finding of microcephaly may suggest several hypotheses, such as cerebral malformation, birth injury, congenital infection, or hypothyroidism. Clinicians can then identify a strategy for testing each hypothesis, which should enable them to determine whether the hypothesis is true. In the example of microcephaly, a hypothesis of cerebral malformation might be supported by a strategy of looking for other malformations or by performing a computed tomographic (CT) scan or magnetic resonance imaging (MRI) study of the brain. A hypothesis of birth injury might be supported by examination of the birth records and evidence that the head circumference was normal at birth. A hypothesis of congenital infection might be supported by serologic evidence of infection with cytomegalovirus, toxoplasmosis, or other agents. A hypothesis of hypothyroidism might be supported by physical evidence of growth failure and by examining the levels of thyroid hormones in the blood. This example is not intended to be a complete analysis of the possible causes of microcephaly. It is described here only to illustrate the process of generating and testing hypotheses regarding possible etiologies.

The purpose of evaluating several competing hypotheses is to optimize the probability of making the correct diagnosis (Elstein, Shulman, and Sprafka, 1978). In some cases, the evaluation of these hypotheses will consist of obtaining additional historical

TABLE 7.2 Hypotheses and Strategies for Determining Etiology

Hypothesis	Possible strategies
I. Prenatal Onset	
A. Chromosomal disorder	Extended physical examination
	Referral to geneticist
	Chromosomal analysis, including fragile X study and high-resolution banding
B. Syndrome disorder	Extended family history and examination of relatives
	Extended physical examination
	Referral to clinical geneticist or neurologist
C. Inborn error of metabolism	Screening for amino acids and organic acids
	Quantification of amino acids in blood, urine, and/or cerebrospinal fluid
	Analysis of organic acids by GC-MS or other methods
	Blood levels of lactate, pyruvate, carnitine, and long-chain fatty acids
	Arterial ammonia and gases
	Assays of specific enzymes
	Biopsies of specific tissue for light and electron microscopic study and biochemical analysis
D. Developmental disorder of brain formation	Computed tomographic (CT) scan of brain
	Magnetic resonance imaging (MRI) scan of the brain

continued

TABLE 7.2 (continued)

Hypothesis	Possible strategies
E. Environmental influence	Growth charts Placental pathology Maternal history and physical examination of mother Toxicological screening of mother at prenatal visits and of child at birth Referral to clinical geneticist
II. Perinatal Onset	Review maternal records (prenatal care, labor, and delivery) Review birth and neonatal records
III. Postnatal Onset	
A. Head injury	Detailed medical history Skull X-rays, CT or MRI scan (for evidence of sequelae)
B. Infection	Detailed medical history
C. Demyelinating disorder	CT or MRI scan
D. Degenerative disorder	CT or MRI scan Evoked potential studies Assays of specific enzymes Biopsy of specific tissue for light and electron microscopy and biochemical analysis
E. Seizure disorder	Electroencephalography
F. Toxic-metabolic disorder	See I.C. on preceding page Toxicological studies, heavy metal assays
G. Malnutrition	Body measurements Detailed nutritional history Family history of nutrition
H. Environmental deprivation	Detailed social history Psychological evaluation Observation in new environment
I. Hypoconnection syndrome	Detailed morphological study of tissue (Huttenlocher, 1991)

information or more extensive physical examination, as described in the preceding example. In many cases, however, the evaluation will necessitate the performance of properly selected laboratory tests and/or procedures. Table 7.2 suggests some laboratory tests and procedures that might be helpful in evaluating the hypotheses listed in the table. This table cannot be considered complete or prescriptive because the evaluation in each case must be tailored to the individual. The clinician is responsible for identifying the appropriate hypotheses, devising strategies for testing them, and evaluating the results of whatever tests and procedures are performed.

No test or procedure should be considered "mandatory" in every case. The evaluation process should be individualized. If the etiology is fairly obvious or if available tests and procedures are not likely to increase the probability of a correct etiologic diagnosis, then no test or procedure may be necessary or indicated. Etiologic evaluation and testing should continue until the most likely etiology has been identified with a reasonable degree of certainty with the information that is available. This may require repeated observations and procedures conducted over a substantial period of time. In some cases, keeping an open mind about the etiology and reconsidering the facts from time to time may yield greater etiologic precision in the future. This approach recognizes the incompleteness of etiological diagnosis in many cases and encourages continued re-evaluation in the light of new information to reach an increasingly close approximation of the actual etiology.

ASSIGNMENT OF THE ETIOLOGY

The purpose of the evaluation and assessment of etiologic data is to assign an etiology that best represents the current understanding of the factors that are responsible for causing mental retardation in that particular individual. This assignment of etiology must specify all of the factors for which sufficient data exist to document their presence or their contribution to the etiology in that individual. If an etiologic factor is suspected but not documented, it may be listed as a "possible" etiology in that case. Inclusion of possible etiologies encourages strategies to obtain additional information (at the present time or in the future) to evaluate the likelihood that this possible etiology is in fact present or contributory. The separation of possible etiologies from those for which sufficient documentation exists avoids potentially unwarranted assumptions about etiology. An example of such an unwarranted assumption would be the listing of "psychosocial disadvantage" as the etiology when a biomedical factor is not apparent, but little or no data exist regarding the psychosocial environment or family functioning. Further investigation is needed in such a case.

If multiple factors are operative, the specification of etiology should indicate the relation among them, if possible. Usually, this means differentiating the primary etiologic factor from whatever secondary factors may have contributed to it. These secondary or contributory factors may include those for which a designation of "possible" is appropriate, as described previously. For example, mental retardation may be caused primarily by brain injury from intracranial hemorrhage at birth. In this example, secondary contributing factors might be premature birth caused by maternal use of cocaine and lack of prenatal care, which may be the result of psychosocial factors such as family disruption and physical abuse. Typically, a listing of multiple etiologic factors would rank them in descending order of importance, with the primary etiology listed first followed by secondary or contributory etiologic factors listed in an order that approximates their relative contribution to the etiology as it is best understood at that time.

CLASSIFICATION AND CODING OF ETIOLOGY

Table 7.3 is a detailed outline of most of the disorders in which mental retardation may occur as a specific manifestation of the disorder. As noted previously, individuals with some of these disorders may not have mental retardation, but the disorder is included in the table if some affected individuals do have mental retardation. Additional information regarding most of these disorders can be found in several texts (Aase, 1990; Buyse, 1990; Jones, 1988). Most of the disorders listed in this table represent biomedical etiologies, but many of them are unusual or rare. In many cases, the primary etiology of an individual with mental retardation will not be one of these specific biomedical disorders. In such cases, it is better to indicate that the etiology is unknown or to list only those psychosocial factors that may be contributory.

Table 7.3 is constructed as an outline to indicate a structural approach that moves from broad, general categories to increasingly specific or homogeneous entities. The broadest category reflects the timing of occurrence of that factor during prenatal, perinatal, or postnatal life. Within each of these categories, secondary groupings include etiologies that are related to each other according to the label indicated. In some instances, a tertiary grouping is indicated to further isolate the specific etiology from others in that category.

The purpose of the outline in Table 7.3 is to allow clinicians to indicate the most specific etiology supported by the data available. In some cases it may be appropriate to indicate only a broad, general category of etiology. This would suggest a need for additional investigation to delineate a more specific etiology within that category. The strategies suggested in Table 7.2 are correlated with these categories of etiology to facilitate such an investigation. Listing the etiology according to the outline in Table 7.3 should help clinicians identify those cases in which more investigation is needed. Subsequent classification of the etiology of mental retardation on Dimension III, informed by the results of such an investigation, might then reflect more precise knowledge regarding the specific disorder or related causal factors involved in that case. The actual listing of etiology on Dimension III should use the outline whenever possible to facilitate comparison between individuals and groups of individuals. The listing should specify each grouping or category. Thus, if the etiology is Rett syndrome, this would be listed as:

Primary Etiology: III.D.1.a, Rett syndrome

In this way, the outline also functions as a coding system for purposes of classification. The advantage of this coding system is that it is based on an understanding of the pathophysiological relations between groups of etiologies, and it is linked to strategies for investigation as suggested in Table 7.2. This will facilitate research on the epidemiology and causes of mental retardation, provide information to public policy developers with regard to the need for services and supports, and assist in the design and implementation of programs to prevent mental retardation.

Medical scientists continue to identify newly recognized entities that may be associated with mental retardation. For example, there are at least three separate clinical patterns of phenylketonuria related to eight distinct abnormalities in the gene involved (Okano, Eisensmith, and Guttler, 1991), and more will undoubtedly be described. Thus, any attempt to list "all" specific etiologies will be outdated by the time it is published. The list in Table 7.3 is currently reasonably complete, but it will become less complete with time. For this reason, the outline in the table is designed so that additional disorders can be added or existing disorders can be subdivided, based on the results of future research. If clinicians wish to code a disorder not included in Table 7.3, the closest code from the table can be used, followed by the designation "ADA" (additional data available). For example, if research shows that there are, in fact, multiple subtypes of Rett syndrome (called types A, B, and C), and if an individual is determined to have the specific subtype called type B, this could be coded as follows:

Primary Diagnosis: III.D.1.a.(ADA), Rett syndrome, type B

Use of the ADA code will be an instruction to those using the codes for classification purposes that greater precision is available and should be included in their work.

Clinicians are often required to use a separate coding system for the purpose of billing for services provided. Several billing systems exist, such as codes provided in the International Classification of Diseases—ICD (World Health Organization, 1978). These coding systems are not designed to increase understanding of the etiology of mental retardation (as the coding system outlined in Table 7.3 is), but their use is a practical necessity in many situations. Clinicians can specify the appropriate diagnostic code for the disorder identified as the etiology of mental retardation, according to whatever coding system (such as the ICD) is required by the particular payor for services rendered in that case. That code can then be used for billing purposes.[1]

---

[1] The most widely used coding system, the International Classification of Diseases—ICD (World Health Organization, in press), is being revised as of the date of publication of this manual, so it is not possible to indicate the new ICD codes for each of the disorders listed in Table 7.3. When these ICD codes become available, a revision of the AAMR Classification of Etiology will be published that specifies both the AAMR code (as described in this chapter) and the most appropriate ICD code for each category, grouping, and specific disorder.

TABLE 7.3 Disorders in Which Mental Retardation May Occur

I. PRENATAL CAUSES

A. Chromosomal Disorders

1. Autosomes
   a. 4p-
   b. Trisomy 4p
   c. Trisomy 8
   d. 5p-
   e. 9p-
   f. Trisomy 9p
   g. Trisomy 9p mosaic
   h. Partial trisomy 10q
   i. 13q-
   j. Ring 13
   k. Trisomy 13 (Patau)
   l. 18p-
   m. 18q-
   n. Trisomy 18 (Edwards)
   o. Trisomy 20p
   p. G (21,22) monosomy/deletion
   q. Trisomy 21 (Down)
   r. Translocation 21   (Down)
   s. "Cat-eye" syndrome

2. X-Linked Mental Retardation
   a. Allan syndrome
   b. Atkin syndrome
   c. Davis syndrome
   d. Fitzsimmons syndrome
   e. Fragile X syndrome
   f. Fragile X phenotype (no fragile site)
   g. Gareis syndrome
   h. Glycerol kinase deficiency
   i. Golabi syndrome
   j. Homes syndrome
   k. Juberg syndrome
   l. Lujan syndrome
   m. Renpenning syndrome
   n. Schimke syndrome
   o. Vasquez syndrome
   p. Nonspecific X-linked mental retardation

3. Other X Chromosome Disorders
   a. XO syndrome (Turner)
   b. XYY syndrome
   c. XXY syndrome (Klinefelter)
   d. XXYY syndrome

continued

TABLE 7.3 (continued)

     e. XXXY syndrome
     f. XXXX syndrome
     g. XXXXY syndrome
     h. XXXXX syndrome (penta-X)

B. Syndrome Disorders

  1. Neurocutaneous Disorders
     a. Ataxia-telangiectasia (Louis-Bar)
     b. Basal cell nevus syndrome
     c. Dyskeratosis congenita
     d. Ectodermal dysplasia, hyperhidrotic type
     e. Ectromelia-ichthyosis syndrome
     f. Focal dermal hypoplasia (Goltz)
     g. Ichthyosis-hypogonadism syndrome
     h. Incontinentia pigmenti (Bloch-Sulzberger)
     i. Ito syndrome
     j. Klippel-Trenauney syndrome
     k. Linear sebaceous nevus syndrome
     l. Multiple lentigines syndrome
     m. Neurofibromatosis (Type 1)
     n. Poikiloderma (Rothmund-Thomsen)
     o. Pollitt syndrome
     p. Sjogren-Larsen syndrome
     q. Sturge-Weber syndrome
     r. Tuberous sclerosis
     s. Xeroderma pigmentosum

  2. Muscular Disorders
     a. Becker muscular dystrophy
     b. Chondrodystrophic myotonia (Schwartz-Jampel)
     c. Congenital muscular dystrophy
     d. Duchenne muscular dystrophy
     e. Myotonic muscular dystrophy

  3. Ocular Disorders
     a. Aniridia-Wilm's tumor syndrome
     b. Anophthalmia syndrome (X-linked)
     c. Leber amaurosis syndrome
     d. Lowe syndrome
     e. Microphthalmia-corneal opacity-spasticity syndrome
     f. Norrie syndrome
     g. Oculocerebral syndrome with hypopigmentation
     h. Retinal degeneration-trichomegaly syndrome
     i. Septo-optic dysplasia

  4. Craniofacial Disorders
     a. Acrocephaly-cleft lip-radial aplasia syndrome
     b. Acrocephalosyndactyly

TABLE 7.3 (continued)

        1. Type 1 (Apert)
        2. Type 2 (Apert)
        3. Type 3 (Saethre-Chotzen)
        4. Type 6 (Pfeiffer)
        5. Carpenter syndrome
        6. With absent digits and cranial defects
    c. Baller-Gerold syndrome
    d. Cephalopolysyndactyly (Greig)
    e. "Cloverleaf-skull" syndrome
    f. Craniofacial dysostosis (Crouzon)
    g. Craniotelencephalic dysplasia
    h. Multiple synostosis syndrome

5. Skeletal Disorders
    a. Acrodysostosis
    b. CHILD syndrome
    c. Chondrodysplasia punctata, Conradi-Hunerman type
    d. Chondroectodermal dysplasia
    e. Dyggve-Melchior-Clausen syndrome
    f. Frontometaphyseal dysplasia
    g. Hereditary osteodystrophy (Albright)
    h. Hyperostosis (Lenz-Majewski)
    i. Hypochondroplasia
    j. Klippel-Feil syndrome
    k. Nail-patella syndrome
    l. Osteopetrosis (Albers-Schonberg)
    m. Pyknodysostosis
    n. Radial aplasia-thrombocytopenia syndrome
    o. Radial hypoplasia-pancytopenia syndrome (Fanconi)
    p. Roberts-SC phocomelia syndrome

6. Other Syndromes
    a. Prader-Willi syndrome

C. Inborn Errors of Metabolism

1. Amino Acid Disorders
    a. Phenylketonuria
        1. Phenylalanine hydroxylase (classical, Type 1)
        2. Dihydropteridine reductase (Type 4)
        3. Dihydrobiopterin synthetase (Type 5)
    b. Histidinemia
    c. Gamma-glutamylcysteine synthetase deficiency
    d. Hyperlysinemia
    e. Lysinuric protein intolerance
    f. Hyperprolinemia
    g. Hydroxyprolinemia
    h. Sulfite oxidase deficiency

TABLE 7.3 (continued)

    i. Iminoglycinuria
    j. Branched-chain amino acid disorders
        1. Hypervalinemia
        2. Hyperleucine-isoleucinemia
        3. Maple-syrup urine disease
        4. Isovaleric acidemia
        5. Glutaric acidemia, Type 2
        6. 3-Hydroxy-3-methylglutaryl CoA lyase deficiency
        7. 3-Ketothiolase deficiency
    k. Biotin-dependent disorders
        1. Holocarboxylase deficiency
        2. Biotinidase deficiency
    l. Propionic acidemia
        1. Type A
        2. Type BC
    m. Methylmalonic acidemia
        1. Mutase type (mut+)
        2. Cofactor affinity type (mut-)
        3. Adenosylcobalamin synthetase type (cbl A)
        4. ATP:cobalamin adenosyltransferase type (cbl B)
        5. With homocystinuria, Type 1 (cbl C)
        6. With homocystinuria, Type 2 (cbl D)
    n. Folate-dependent disorders
        1. Congenital defect of folate absorption
        2. Dihydrofolate reductase deficiency
        3. Methylene tetrahydrofolate reductase deficiency
    o. Homocystinuria
    p. Hypersarcosinemia
    q. Non-ketotic hyperglycinemia
    r. Hyper-beta-alaninemia
    s. Carnosinase deficiency
    t. Homocarnosinase deficiency
    u. Hartnup disease
    v. Methionine malabsorption (oasthouse urine disease)

2. Carbohydrate Disorders
    a. Glycogen storage disorders
        1. Type 1, with hypoglycemia (von Gierke)
        2. Type 2 (Pompe)
    b. Galactosemia
    c. Fructose-1, 6-diphosphatase deficiency
    d. Pyruvic acid disorders
        1. Pyruvate dehydrogenase complex (Leigh)
        2. Pyruvate carboxylase deficiency

TABLE 7.3 (continued)

  e. Mannosidosis
  f. Fucosidosis
  g. Aspartylglucosaminuria

3. Mucopolysaccharide Disorders
  a. Alpha-L-iduronidase deficiency
    1. Hurler type
    2. Scheie type
    3. Hurler–Scheie type
  b. Iduronate sulfatase deficiency (Hunter type)
  c. Heparan N-sulfatase deficiency (Sanfilippo 3A type)
  d. N-acetyl-alpha-D-glucosaminidase deficiency (Sanfilippo 3B type)
  e. Acetyl CoA: glucosaminide N-acetyltransferase deficiency (Sanfilippo 3C type)
  f. N-acetyl-alpha D-glucosaminide 6-sulfatase deficiency (Sanfilippo 3D type)
  g. Beta-glucuronidase deficiency (Sly type)

4. Mucolipid Disorders
  a. Alpha-neuraminidase deficiency (Type 1)
  b. N-acetylglucosaminyl phosphotransferase deficiency
    1. I-cell disease (Type 2)
    2. Pseudo-Hurler syndrome (Type 3)
  c. Mucolipidosis Type 4

5. Urea Cycle Disorders
  a. Carbamyl phosphate synthetase deficiency
  b. Ornithine transcarbamylase deficiency
  c. Argininosuccinic acid synthetase deficiency (citrullinemia)
  d. Argininosuccinic acid (ASA) lyase deficiency
  e. Arginase deficiency (argininemia)

6. Nucleic Acid Disorders
  a. Lesch-Nyhan syndrome (HGPRTase deficiency)
  b. Orotic aciduria
  c. Xeroderma pigmentosum, group A
  d. DeSanctis-Cacchione syndrome

7. Copper Metabolism Disorders
  a. Wilson disease
  b. Menkes disease

8. Mitochondrial Disorders
  a. Kearns-Sayre syndrome
  b. MELAS syndrome
  c. MERRF syndrome
  d. Cytochrome c oxidase deficiency
  e. Other mitochondrial disorders

9. Peroxisomal Disorders
  a. Zellweger syndrome

TABLE 7.3 (continued)

b. Adrenoleukodystrophy
 1. Neonatal (autosomal recessive)
 2. Childhood (X-linked)
c. Infantile Refsum disease
d. Hyperpipecolic acidemia
e. Chondrodysplasia punctata, rhizomelic type

D. Developmental Disorders of Brain Formation

1. Neural Tube Closure Defects
 a. Anencephaly
 b. Spina bifida
 c. Encephalocele

2. Brain Formation Defects
 a. Dandy-Walker malformation
 b. Holoprosencephaly
 c. Hydrocephalus
 1. Aqueductal stenosis
 2. Congenital X-linked type
 d. Lissencephaly
 e. Pachygyria
 f. Polymicrogyria
 g. Schizencephaly

3. Cellular Migration Defects
 a. Abnormal layering of cortex
 b. Colpocephaly
 c. Heterotopias of gray matter
 d. Cortical microdysgenesis

4. Intraneuronal Defects
 a. Dendritic spine abnormalities
 b. Microtubule abnormalities

5. Acquired Brain Defects
 a. Hydranencephaly
 b. Porencephaly

6. Primary (Idiopathic) Microcephaly

E. Environmental Influences

1. Intrauterine Malnutrition
 a. Maternal malnutrition
 b. Placental insufficiency (see Perinatal)

2. Drugs, Toxins, and Teratogens
 a. Thalidomide
 b. Aminopterin

TABLE 7.3 (continued)

c. Warfarin
d. Trimethadione
e. Phenytoin (fetal hydantoin syndrome)
f. Alcohol (fetal alcohol syndrome)
g. Narcotics
h. Cocaine
i. Methylmercury

3. Maternal Diseases
a. Hyperthermia
b. Varicella
c. Diabetes mellitus
d. Hypothyroidism (fetal iodine deficiency)
e. Maternal myotonic dystrophy
f. Maternal phenylketonuria

4. Irradiation During Pregnancy

F. Other (nonspecific, unknown)

II. PERINATAL CAUSES

A. Intrauterine Disorders

1. Acute Placental Insufficiency
a. Abruptio placentae
b. Placenta previa/hemorrhage
c. Maternal hypotension
d. Toxemia/eclampsia
e. Twin–twin transfusion

2. Chronic Placental Insufficiency (marginal reserve)
a. Maternal hypertension (placental infarcts)
b. Intrauterine growth retardation (small for dates)
c. Postmaturity (involution)
d. Erythroblastosis (edema)
e. Maternal anemia
f. Maternal diabetes

3. Abnormal Labor and Delivery
a. Premature labor (prematurity)
b. Premature rupture of membranes
c. Prolonged rupture of membranes and amnionitis
d. Maternal sepsis
e. Abnormal presentation (especially breech)
f. Delayed second stage (cephalopelvic disproportion)
g. Umbilical cord prolapse
h. Umbilical cord accidents (nuchal cord, knot, avulsion)
i. Obstetrical trauma

4. Multiple Gestation (smaller, later, or male infant)

TABLE 7.3 (continued)

B. Neonatal Disorders

1. Hypoxic-Ischemic Encephalopathy

2. Intracranial Hemorrhage
   a. Subdural
   b. Subarachnoid
   c. Parenchymal
   d. Intraventricular
   e. Cerebellar
   f. Brainstem

3. Posthemorrhagic Hydrocephalus

4. Periventricular Leukomalacia

5. Neonatal Seizures

6. Respiratory Disorders
   a. Hyaline membrane disease
   b. Bronchopulmonary dysplasia (chronic hypoxia)
   c. Pneumothorax (acute hypoxia)

7. Infections
   a. Septicemia
   b. Meningitis
      1. Enterobacter sakazaki
      2. Escherichia coli
      3. Streptococcus (group B and others)
      4. Other meningitis
   c. Encephalitis
      1. Cytomegalovirus
      2. Herpes simplex
      3. Human immunodeficiency virus
      4. Rubella
      5. Syphilis
      6. Toxoplasmosis

8. Head Trauma at Birth

9. Metabolic Disorders
   a. Hyperbilirubinemia (kernicterus)
   b. Hypoglycemia
   c. Hypothyroidism
   d. Inborn errors of metabolism (neonatal onset)

10. Nutritional Disorders
    a. Intestinal disorders
    b. Protein-calorie malnutrition

TABLE 7.3 (continued)

III. POSTNATAL CAUSES

A. Head Injuries

1. Cerebral concussion (diffuse axonal injury)
2. Cerebral contusion or laceration
3. Intracranial hemorrhage
   a. Epidural (tentorial herniation)
   b. Acute subdural (with diffuse injury)
   c. Chronic subdural
4. Subarachnoid (with diffuse injury)
5. Parenchymal

B. Infections

1. Encephalitis
   a. Herpes simplex
   b. Measles
   c. Arbovirus
   d. Human immunodeficiency virus
2. Meningitis
   a. Streptococcus pneumoniae
   b. Neisseria meningitidis
   c. Hemophilus influenzae, type B
   d. Mycobacterium tuberculosis
3. Fungal Infections
4. Parasitic Infestations
   a. Cysticercosis
   b. Malaria
5. Slow or Persistent Virus Infections
   a. Measles (Subacute sclerosing panencephalitis)
   b. Rubella (Progressive rubella panencephalitis)

C. Demyelinating Disorders

1. Postinfectious Disorders
   a. Acute disseminated encephalomyelitis
   b. Acute hemorrhagic encephalomyelitis
2. Postimmunization Disorders
   a. Post-pertussis encephalopathy
3. Schilder Disease

D. Degenerative Disorders

1. Syndromic Disorders
   a. Rett syndrome
   b. Disintegrative psychosis (Heller)

TABLE 7.3 (continued)

2. Poliodystrophies
   a. Alpers disease
   b. Infantile neuroaxonal dystrophy
   c. Friedreich ataxia
   d. Progressive myoclonus epilepsy
      1. Unverricht-Lundborg type
      2. Lafora body type
      3. Baltic type

3. Basal Ganglia Disorders
   a. Hallervorden-Spatz disease
   b. Huntington disease (juvenile type)
   c. Parkinson disease (juvenile type)
   d. Fahr disease
   e. Dystonia musculorum deformans
   f. Familial striatal necrosis
   g. Pallidal atrophy-choreoathetosis syndrome

4. Leukodystrophies
   a. Alexander disease
   b. Cockayne syndrome
   c. Canavan disease
   d. Pelizaeus-Merzbacher disease
   e. Sudanophilic leukodystrophy
   f. Ceroid lipofuchsinosis
      1. Congenital (Santavuori-Hagberg)
      2. Late infantile type (Batten-Bielschowsky-Jansky)
      3. Juvenile type (Spielmeyer-Vogt)
      4. Late onset type (Kufs)
   g. Adrenoleukodystrophy
      1. Neonatal (autosomal recessive)
      2. Childhood (X-linked)
   h. Galactosylceramidase deficiency (Krabbe)
   i. Arylsulfatase A deficiency (metachromatic leukodystrophy)
   j. Multiple sulfatase deficiency

5. Sphingolipid Disorders
   a. Ceramidase deficiency (Farber)
   b. Beta-galactosidase deficiency (GM1 gangliosidosis)
      1. Type 1 (generalized)
      2. Type 2 (cerebral)
   c. Hexosaminidase A deficiency (Tay-Sachs)
   d. Hexosaminidase A and B deficiency (Sandhoff)
   e. Glucocerebrosidase deficiency (Gaucher)
   f. Sphingomyelinase deficiency (Niemann-Pick)
   g. Alpha-galactosidase deficiency (Fabry)

6. Other Lipid Disorders

TABLE 7.3 (continued)

    a. Acid lipase deficiency (Wolman)
    b. Juvenile dystonic lipidosis
    c. Cerebrotendinous xanthomatosis
    d. Abetalipoproteinemia (Bassen-Kornzweig)

E. Seizure Disorders

1. Infantile Spasms

2. Myoclonic Epilepsy
    a. Early infantile type
    b. Late infantile type
    c. Myoclonic-astatic type

3. Lennox-Gastaut Syndrome

4. Progressive Focal Epilepsy (Rasmussen)

5. Status epilepticus-induced brain injury

F. Toxic-Metabolic Disorders

1. Acute Toxic Encephalopathy

2. Reye Syndrome

3. Intoxications
    a. Lead
    b. Mercury

4. Metabolic Disorders
    a. Dehydration
    b. Cerebral ischemia
    c. Cerebral anoxia
    d. Hypoglycemia
    e. Inborn errors of metabolism (childhood onset)

G. Malnutrition

1. Protein-Calorie (PCM)
    a. Kwashiorkor
    b. Marasmus
    c. Chronic moderate-degree PCM
    d. Intergenerational effect

2. Prolonged Intravenous Alimentation

H. Environmental Deprivation

1. Psychosocial Disadvantage

2. Child Abuse and Neglect

3. Chronic Social/Sensory Deprivation

I. Hypoconnection Syndrome

CHAPTER 8

DIMENSION IV:
ENVIRONMENTAL CONSIDERATIONS

Dimension IV of the Definition, Classification, and Systems of Supports focuses on the person's environment and the significant influence that environments have on behavioral development and expression. Users of the manual are asked in this chapter to consider:

- The specific settings in which the person receives educational services, lives, and/or works
- The extent to which the characteristics of these environments facilitate or restrict factors that influence a person's growth, development, and well-being
- The optimum environment that would facilitate the person's independence/ interdependence, productivity, community integration, social belonging, and well-being

There are four simple questions asked frequently regarding the quality of service for individuals with mental retardation: What is the person doing? Where is he or she doing it? When is the person doing it? With whom? These questions and their answers reflect the importance of activities, environments, and relationships. They also emphasize the importance of considering environments in a multidimensional classification system. To that end, this chapter is divided into three sections: (a) a brief discussion of the importance of environments, (b) the characteristics of wholesome environments, and (c) the analysis of environments.

IMPORTANCE OF ENVIRONMENTS

Numerous reports support the significant role that environments can have in fostering positive behavioral growth and development (Edgerton, 1988; Fine, Tangeman, and Woodard, 1990; Garber, 1988; Landesman and Ramey, 1989; Perske, 1988). The current situation was summarized well by Baumeister (1987):

> . . . given recent developments in the social-legal sphere together with a greatly enlarged scientific knowledge base, we can expect increasing pressure to fundamentally revise our conceptions of mental retardation. This will lead to new methods for valid diagnosis and classification. We can anticipate that classification systems will emerge with a much more balanced emphasis on both the individual and the demands and constraints of specific environments. (pp. 799–800)

CHARACTERISTICS OF WHOLESOME ENVIRONMENTS

A major part of the reconceptualization is the current focus on environmental characteristics that can either facilitate or hinder a person's growth, development, well-being, and
satisfaction. As shown in Figure 8.1, wholesome environments have three major characteristics: providing opportunities, fostering well-being, and promoting stability (Schalock
and Kiernan, 1990).

PROVIDE OPPORTUNITIES

A basic truism is that "you cannot benefit from an opportunity you've never had."
Providing opportunities to people with mental retardation is one of our most important
challenges and tasks. Providing education, living, work, and recreation–leisure services
and supports in integrated settings creates situations that stimulate the person to grow
and develop. Community-based integrated opportunities and wholesome environments
can provide (Knoll, 1990, Perske, 1988; Schalock, 1990; Smull, 1990):

- An enhanced satisfaction with one's life
- A sense of love, affection, and belonging that comes from loving relationships
  and friendships
- A sense of security that comes from self-control and control over one's
  environment
- Enhanced choice, opportunity, and control

Figure 8.1 Qualities of Wholesome Environments

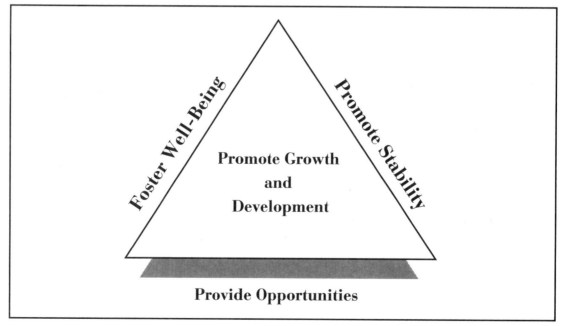

94

FOSTER WELL-BEING

Recent efforts to identify factors within an individual's environment that foster and enhance his or her well-being suggest the more important of these factors are (Blunden, 1988; Flanagan, 1978; Schalock and Kiernan, 1990):

- Physical, including health and personal safety
- Material, including material comforts and financial security
- Social, including community and civic activities
- Leisure and recreation within a wellness perspective
- Cognitive stimulation and development
- Work that is interesting, rewarding, and worthwhile

PROMOTE STABILITY

One of the most important aspects of any environment is its quality of stability, with associated aspects of predictability and control. The importance of such stability is supported by the demonstrated relation between stability and enhanced learning, positive emotional affiliation, facilitative social support systems, and reduced stress (Schalock and Kiernan, 1990). It is important to realize that the promotion of environmental stability often coexists in tension with one's commitment to opportunities for growth and development. Therefore, as described more fully in chapter 9, the intensities of supports provided to a person may vary over the life span as new opportunities arise in the world of work, living, and personal growth (Nisbet and Hagner, 1988).

Table 8.1 lists a number of ways in which environments can be modified to enhance a person's sense of well-being and stability. The suggestions are organized around the four life areas—physical, material, social, and cognitive.

ANALYZING ENVIRONMENTS

As mentioned previously, Dimension IV of the 1992 AAMR Definition, Classification, and Systems of Supports describes settings in which a person receives educational services, lives, and/or works. A part of that analysis is the evaluation of the environment's characteristics across a number of factors related to the individual's personal growth, development, and enhanced life satisfaction. The following discussion concerns two aspects of that analysis.

CURRENT SETTING

In describing the person's current setting, one might find the checklist presented in Table 8.2 to be useful. In completing this table, keep in mind that during a person's early years, the primary environments are home and school. Table 8.2 requires evaluation of the person's current education–living–employment environment in response to four critical variables: (a) level of integration, (b) level of participation, (c) intensities of needed supports, and (d) hours of service per month.

TABLE 8.1   Environmental Factors That Enhance a Person's Sense of Well-Being and Stability

Life area	Factor	Suggestions to maximize factor
Physical	Health, fitness, nutrition	Safeguard the person's health and fitness Ensure adequate medical, dental, optical, physical therapy, and nutritional services
Material	Housing, possessions, income	Allow ownership and control of one's material possessions Maximize the amount of disposable income that is under the person's control Safeguard and promote the physical quality of the home Promote quantity and quality of person's possessions
Social	Community presence	Promote access to community, such as shops, leisure facilities, and places of education Encourage a range of friends, family members, colleagues, and peers Allow choices over home, activities, possessions, and activities Develop basic abilities in communication, ability, self-help, and social leisure skills Use prosthetics and environmental accommodation techniques Stress and allow for valued social roles and activities
Cognitive	Cognitive development	Provide stimulation, education, and enriched environments Teach decision-making skills Allow choices and decision-making Develop competence and allow for choices and decision

Note: Adapted from Blunden (1988), O'Brien (1987), and Schalock and Kiernan (1990).

TABLE 8.2 Factors to Consider in Evaluating the Person's Current Setting

Current Settings	Level of integration			Level of participation			Intensities of supports				Hours of service per month
	Full	Partial	None	High	Medium	Low	Intermittent	Limited	Extensive	Pervasive	
Educational/habilitation program											
Public education (community college, GED,[a] continuing education)											
MR/DD related education/ habilitation services											
No formal education/ habilitation services											
Living environment											
Independent (rents/owns home)											
Semi-independent (in a home setting, but with some supervision)											
Supervised (e.g., group home)											
Specialized facility (hospital, nursing home, institution)											
Employment environment											
Regular employment (self-employed, part-time, full-time)											
Employed, but receiving ongoing support											
Sheltered/segregated work (e.g., sheltered workshop)											
Unemployed (check one)											
— not seeking employment (e.g., homemaker)											
— seeking or has sought employment											
Retired											

[a]General Education Degree.

CHARACTERISTICS OF OPTIMUM ENVIRONMENTS

There are numerous ways that environments can be analyzed and their optimum characteristics described. The method proposed here evaluates an environment according to the opportunities afforded by that environment to increase the individual's independence/interdependence, productivity, community integration, and satisfaction. Five optimum environmental characteristics to evaluate are:

- *Community Presence*: the sharing of the ordinary places that define community life
- *Choice*: the experience of autonomy, decision-making, and control
- *Competence*: the opportunity to learn and perform functional and meaningful activities
- *Respect*: the reality of having a valued place in one's community
- *Community Participation*: the experience of being part of a growing network of family and friends (O'Brien, 1987).

Evaluating these environmental characteristics requires observing a person in his or her environment and answering questions related to what the person is doing, where he or she is doing it, when the person is doing it, with whom the person is doing it, and what else the person wishes to do or do more of. It also requires analyzing the person's current education, living, and employment environments to determine what environmental conditions are either facilitating or inhibiting these factors.

The format provided in Table 8.3 will assist in this evaluation. For example, Joe's Individual Program Plan (IPP) team recently met and completed this table with Joe's input. Factors that facilitated community presence included Joe's frequent shopping and recreational activities. His presence was inhibited by his nonambulatory status and consequent need for a stand-by personal assistant. Joe's choices were facilitated by his stated desires of involvement in activities and group membership. There did not seem to be any inhibiting factors in his choices. In fact, he recently refused to sign his IPP until certain changes were made in his payee status. Joe's competence was enhanced through the use of kitchen and laundry adaptations that permitted him to live in his own home and telecommunication devices that allowed him to wear a "med alert" should he need assistance during the night. His competence is still inhibited because of lack of a modified van for easier access to his job. Joe has earned the respect of his co-workers and friends but feels that "I must be more mobile before I have my own full respect." His community participation is facilitated through job and activities but is inhibited somewhat without a stand-up ambulatory aid that will allow dancing. Such an evaluation of Joe's environment and his personal goals was productive and led the team to think about accessing some of the environmentally based supports discussed in the next chapter.

In summary, in this chapter the importance of environments to one's personal growth and development has been stressed. We have also suggested methods that one can use to describe a person's current setting and evaluate the environmental characteristics that either facilitate or inhibit the person's well-being and life satisfaction. Once the evaluation is made, supports should come into play. Factors to consider in using supports are discussed in the next chapter.

TABLE 8.3 Optimal Environmental Factors

Factor	Environmental conditions	
	Facilitate factor	Inhibit factor
1. Community Presence		
2. Choice		
3. Competence		
4. Respect		
5. Community Participation		

CHAPTER 9

APPROPRIATE SUPPORTS

There is currently considerable conceptual and practical interest in the use of natural supports as an efficient and effective way to maximize habilitation services to individuals with disabilities. Although the concept of natural supports is by no means new, what *is* new is the belief that the judicious application of appropriate supports can improve the functional capabilities of individuals with mental retardation. This belief is exemplified in the current emphasis on supported employment, supported living, and regular-class support systems in education. The importance of supports is that they hold the promise of providing a more natural, efficient, and on-going basis for enhancing a person's independence/interdependence, productivity, community integration, and satisfaction.

The heightened interest in natural supports comes at a critical time. For example, we are just now implementing the Americans with Disabilities Act of 1990 (PL 101-336), which draws the nation's attention to the 43 million Americans who have one or more physical or mental disabilities. In addition, the rehabilitation profession is currently experiencing a significant paradigmatic shift characterized by:

- A "quality" revolution, with its emphasis on personal life satisfaction, quality enhancement techniques, and quality assurance
- A consumer-referenced goal of personal growth and development, emphasizing choices, decisions, and empowerment
- An increasing need for fiscal and programmatic accountability
- The provision of services in natural environments, based on the principles of real jobs and real homes, the community good, and natural supports

Step 3 of the Definition, Classification, and Systems of Supports focuses on the specific needed supports of the individual. In brief, the third step involves determining needed supports for individuals with mental retardation across the four dimensions. Based on that determination, the individual's intensities of needed supports could be classified as intermittent, limited, extensive, or pervasive (see Table 3.1).

The purpose of the present chapter is to expand on and operationalize the concept of supports and to outline a procedure for determining specific needed supports for individuals with mental retardation. The chapter is divided into three sections: (a) support resources, functions, intensities, and desired outcomes; (b) the determination of needed intensities of supports; and (c) implications of using supports. Throughout the chapter, *supports* are defined as

> resources and strategies that promote the interests and causes of individuals with or without disabilities; that enable them to access resources, information, and relationships inherent within integrated work and living environments; and that result in their enhanced interdependence/interdependence, productivity, community integration, and satisfaction.

Note the three key aspects of supports. First, they pertain to resources and strategies; second, they enable individuals to access resources, information, and relationships within integrated environments; and third, their use results in increased integration and enhanced personal growth and development.

SUPPORT RESOURCES, FUNCTIONS, INTENSITIES, AND DESIRED OUTCOMES

The current conceptual and practical interest in the use of supports extends across disciplines and habilitation areas, including education (Haring and Breen, 1989), families (Roberts, Wasik, Casto, and Ramey, 1991), employment (Hughes, Rusch, and Curl, 1990; Nisbet and Hagner, 1988), and medicine (Coulter, 1991; Parette, Hourcade, and Brimberry, 1990). In addition, the current emphasis on supports and systems of supports is consistent with the 19th century concept of *communitarianism* (that is, tempering the excesses of individualism with an assertion of the rights of others in the larger society) and the current public policy emphasis on quality (H. Turnbull and Brunk, 1990). Thus, although a currently popular topic, the concept of supports is by no means a new one. What is new, however, is the belief that the judicious application of appropriate supports can improve the functional capabilities of individuals with disabilities.

There are currently a number of ways to conceptualize the source of supports, along with their functions, intensities, and desired outcomes. The model that is used in this chapter is shown in Figure 9.1. The four components of the model are support resources, support functions, intensities of supports, and desired outcomes.

FIGURE 9.1. **Supports–Outcome Model**

Support Resources	Support Functions		Intensities of Supports
• Personal	• Befriending	• In-Home Living Assistance	• Intermittent
• Other People	• Financial Planning	• Community Access and Use	• Limited
• Technology			• Extensive
• Services	• Employee Assistance	• Health Assistance	• Pervasive
	• Behavioral Support		

Desired Outcomes
• Enhance Adaptive Skills Level/Functional Capabilities
• Maximize Habilitation Goals Related to Health, Physical, Psychological, or Functional Wellness
• Foster Environmental Characteristics of Community Presence, Choice, Competence, Respect, Community Participation

SUPPORT RESOURCES

Supports can come from a number of resources, including oneself, other people (Perske, 1988), technology, and habilitation services. The following are examples of each type of support.

- *Individual*: skills, competencies, the ability and opportunity to make choices, money, information, spiritual values
- *Other People*: family, friends, co-workers, co-habitants, mentors
- *Technology*: assistive devices, job/living accommodations, behavioral technology
- *Services*: currently available habilitation services that are to be used if natural resources are not available

SUPPORT FUNCTIONS

The resources and strategies referenced in the definition can be grouped into seven support functions for the purposes of conceptualization and providing the basis for assessment activities: befriending, financial planning, employee assistance, behavioral support, in-home living assistance, community access and use, and health assistance. Representative activities associated with each support function are summarized in Table 9.1.

There are three key points to consider relative to the support functions listed in Table 9.1. First, the major purpose of supports is to enhance successful integration. Therefore, we should strive to use natural supports whenever possible. Second, supports may either be of life-long duration or their need may fluctuate during different life stages. Third, supportive services should not be withdrawn unless the service provider continues to monitor the person's current and future needs for supports.

SUPPORT INTENSITIES

Support intensity needs vary across people, situations, and life stages. Hence, supports should be viewed as varying potentially in both duration and intensity. In reference to intensity, the AAMR classification system suggests the four support intensities defined in chapter 3: intermittent, limited, extensive, and pervasive (see Table 3.1 for definitions and examples of intensities of supports).

DESIRED OUTCOMES

Figure 9.1 lists three desired outcomes from the use of supports. Additional desired outcomes include:

- Contributing to personal, social, and emotional development
- Strengthening self-esteem and individual sense of worth
- Offering opportunities to make contributions

TABLE 9.1 Support Functions and Representative Activities

Support function[a]	Representative activities		
Befriending	Advocating	Evaluating	Befriending
	Car pooling	Communicating	Associating
	Supervising	Training	Collecting data
	Instructing	Giving feedback	Socializing
Financial planning	Working with SSI-Medicaid	Assisting with money management	Budgeting
	Advocating for benefits	Protection and legal assistance	Income assistance and planning/considerations
Employee assistance	Counseling	Supervisory training	Crisis intervention/assistance
	Procuring/using assistive technology devices	Job performance enhancement	Job/task accommodation and redesigning job/work duties
Behavioral support	Functional analysis	Manipulation of ecological and setting events	Building environment with effective consequences and minimizing the use of punishers
	Multicomponent instruction	Teaching adaptive behavior	
	Emphasis on antecedent manipulation		
In-Home living assistance	Personal Maintenance/Care	Communication devices	Respite care
	Transfer and mobility	Behavioral support	Attendant care
	Dressing and clothing care	Eating & food management	Homehealth aides
	Architectural modifications	Housekeeping	Homemaker services and med alert devices
Community access and use	Carpooling/rides program	Recreation/leisure involvement	Community use opportunities and interacting with generic agencies
	Transportation training	Community awareness opportunities	
		Vehicle modification	
Health assistance	Medical appointments	Emergency procedures	Hazard awareness
	Medical interventions	Mobility (assistive devices)	Safety training
	Supervision	Counseling appointments	Physical therapy and related activities and
	Med Alert devices	Medication taking	Counseling interventions

Note: Adapted from Googins (1989); Horner et al. (1990); Hughes et al. (1990); Koehler, Schalock, and Ballard (1989); Kierman and McGaughey (1991); Meador, Osborn, Owens, Smith, and Taylor (1991); Nisbet and Hagner (1988); Powell et al. (1991); Roberts et al. (1991); Schalock and Kiernan (1990); Schalock and Koehler (1988); and Temple University (1990).

[a]The support functions and activities may need to be modified slightly to accommodate individuals of different ages.

DETERMINATION OF NEEDED INTENSITIES OF SUPPORTS

Table 9.2 provides a working model for determining a person's needed types and intensities of supports. The first column lists those adaptive skill areas referenced in the definition and whose assessment was discussed in chapter 4. It also lists general habilitation goal areas represented by Dimensions II (Psychological/Emotional Considerations) and III (Physical/Health/Etiology Considerations), which were discussed in chapters 5, 6, and 7. The last heading in Column 1 contains those significant characteristics that reflect the environmental considerations discussed in chapter 8.

The second column requires clinicians to specify the support resource(s) most appropriate to an individual's needs. Again, it is important to emphasize that in addition to coming from other people, technical devices, and services, resources can be personal and, thus, come from the individual. This focus on the individual as a resource is consistent with the current emphasis on personal empowerment, decision-making, and choices.

The third column requires the team to determine—for each focus area in Column 1 where there is a need—the appropriate intensities of needed supports.

The fourth column asks clinicians to identify the basis for the determination. This step is important because it allows the interdisciplinary team to integrate all relevant assessment information and to verify its source and inclusion in the implementation process. Note here that the intensities of supports can be determined at least in part by the person with mental retardation, who is frequently in the best position to make that determination. The determination of needed supports can also be made on the basis of behavioral observation and/or clinical assessments.

The final column of Table 9.2 requires a listing of specific supports, which include those support functions and specific activities listed in Table 9.1.

In summary, the determination of the needed intensities and types of supports represents a synthesis of the multidimensional Definition, Classification, and Systems of Supports. The process also provides rationales and explanations for the implementation of the four assumptions that are essential to the application of the definition of mental retardation:

1. Valid assessment considers cultural and linguistic diversity as well as differences in communication and behavioral factors;

2. The existence of limitations in adaptive skills occurs within the context of community environments typical of the individual's age peers and is indexed to the person's individualized needs for supports;

3. Specific adaptive limitations often coexist with strengths in other adaptive skills or other personal capabilities; and

4. With appropriate supports over a sustained period, the life functioning of the person with mental retardation will generally improve.

Table 9.2 Support Planning Matrix

Support focus area	Support resource		Support intensities				Basis for determination			Specific supports[a]
	Personal Other people	Technical	Intermittent	Limited	Extensive	Pervasive	Person's input	Behavioral observation	Clinical assessment	
Adaptive skills										
Communication										
Self-care										
Social skills										
Home living										
Community use										
Self-direction										
Health & safety										
Functional academics										
Leisure										
Work										
Habilitation goals										
Psychological/emotional										
Health										
Physical										
Environmental characteristics										
Community presence										
Choice										
Competence										
Respect										
Community participation										

[a]Such as those functions listed in Table 9.1.

IMPLICATIONS OF USING SUPPORTS

The concept of supports and their use with individuals who have mental retardation is just emerging in the field. Therefore, the five implications regarding the use of supports discussed in this section are based on our current understanding and may well change over time.

The first implication relates to the assumption that states "with appropriate supports over a sustained period, the life functioning of the person with mental retardation will generally improve." The positive aspect of this statement is that many individuals diagnosed as having mental retardation frequently "outgrow" their need for both the label and the formalized services being offered. For a large percentage of such persons, their desire is to cease being considered as having mental retardation, and, unfortunately, the services provide the rationale for the label. The potential negative aspect of these statements is that some individuals may lose necessary services when their functioning level exceeds an arbitrary criterion allegedly justifying that support is no longer needed. Another potential negative impact might involve the individual's miscalculation of his or her ability and overestimation of ability to function without support. These possible scenarios underlie the caution and professional competence that should guide the use of supports and prevent their premature withdrawal. Inherent in this caution is the acknowledgement that individuals can "move in and out" of different types and intensities of supports and systems of supports.

The second implication relates to the need to distinguish between those "training and treatment efforts" that are designed primarily to improve the individual's intrinsic skills and those environmental and social accommodations that reduce the consequences of the condition. Even though there is an overlap, a conceptual distinction needs to be made. According to Elizabeth Boggs (personal communication, 1991):

> This is important theoretically but also practically. Capacity or compe-
> tence, if developed or restored through training or treatment, belongs
> to the individual and may in fact reduce disability (and even in some
> cases impairment). Environmental modifications and personal support
> services facilitate function while present but do not reduce the intrinsic
> disability. This fact should not be obscured as long as the individual can/
> will once more experience the consequences of his functional disability
> if he moves out of the special environment or loses the personal support.

The distinction is of critical importance in determining or maintaining legitimate eligibility and is discussed in more detail in chapter 12.

The third implication relates to the emerging technology of support. In a recent review, Bellamy (1990) suggested that the following features appear to be critical in a technology of support:

1. The technology should blend public and private sources of support in a coherent, manageable model.

2. Ongoing support should address assistance needs in all parts of a person's life.

3. Models for providing ongoing support should reflect realistic cost constraints.

4.   Support should enhance opportunities for integration and participation.

5.   Support should be linked to measures of individual benefits and outcomes.

A fourth implication of supports is associated with recognition of the significant role of spiritual beliefs and their expression in the lives of people with mental retardation, as its importance is increasingly acknowledged for all individuals (Naisbitt and Aburdene, 1990). Acceptance and inclusion in the spiritual life of the community is an important source of support that is frequently overlooked for individuals with mental retardation.

The variety of ways in which people with mental retardation express spiritual beliefs parallels that of the general population. They include compliance with expected religious behavior and active participation in religious activities. They also include the expression of more general or universal beliefs that need not be linked to any particular religious activity. These beliefs may form the basis of the person's values, which then help to guide his or her moral behavior (Coulter, 1991a).

Spiritual awareness is only marginally related to intelligence, if at all. Indeed, the argument has been made that spirituality constitutes a dimension of human life that is separate from the physical and mental dimension (Nelson, 1984). According to this argument, intelligence is part of the mental dimension while the spiritual dimension includes friendship, love, and prayer. The ability to accept or deny a personal relationship with God (or a comparable concept of a divine being beyond human knowledge) is an important aspect of this spiritual dimension of human life (Coulter, 1991a). It is the ability to choose, not the actual acceptance or denial of such a relationship, that is critical to human life.

These considerations lead to the conclusion that spiritual awareness can be an integrating experience, an experience of inclusion in the community. It is an experience that can be shared by families that include a member with mental retardation, and this sharing helps to develop the spiritual awareness of individuals with mental retardation as it does for all family members (Coulter, 1990). Furthermore, it is an experience of acceptance (for example, in the larger religious community) that may be lacking in other important areas of the life of individuals with mental retardation. The benefits of this experience of acceptance are illustrated by the frequent observation that self-esteem and interpersonal behavior may improve when people with mental retardation are included in a religious community.

The final implication relates to support standards. Because the use of natural supports is just emerging in the habilitation field, one needs to consider carefully the standards that guide their development and use. This is especially true because accreditation and licensing/certification standards currently focus primarily on services that are driven by the individual habilitation planning process. The assumption underlying these standards is that current habilitation programs should be offered through a structured, multi-disciplinary program planning process. There are currently no comparable standards for support programs because support services frequently do not require the level of structure or intensity of typical habilitation programs (Pearce, 1990). However, there is still a need for developing standards to guide the assessment and use of natural supports. Seven proposed natural supports standards are:

1. Natural supports occur in regular, integrated environments.

2. Support activities are performed primarily by individuals normally working, living, or recreating within that environment.

3. Support activities are individualized and person-referenced.

4. Natural supports are coordinated through a person such as a supports manager.

5. Outcomes from the use of natural supports are evaluated against quality indicators and person-referenced outcomes.

6. The use of supports can fluctuate, and may range from life-long duration to fluctuating need during different stages of life.

7. Supports should not be withdrawn unless the service provider continues to monitor the person's current and future intensities of need for supports.

Although these standards may change over time, they seem reasonable to use at this point to evaluate the presence and quality of the natural supports used.

In summary, the concept of supports and their use is integral to the definition of mental retardation that incorporates the possible nonpermanent nature of mental retardation and the demonstrated fact that with appropriate supports over a sustained period, the life functioning of individuals with mental retardation will generally improve. In this chapter we have described the judicious and effective use of supports for individuals with mental retardation. The material presented outlined a supports–outcome model reflecting support resources, support functions, intensities of supports, and the desired outcomes from the use of supports. In addition, a procedure was described that allows clinicians to determine the intensities and specific types of supports needed. We noted that it may be easier for a service provider offering a single service to determine the individual's intensities of needed supports; the process of determining support intensities is more difficult when multiple service providers are involved. However, as was stressed throughout the chapter, the significance of providing supports to individuals with mental retardation is that their use will provide a more natural, efficient, and ongoing basis for enhancing growth, development, and life satisfaction.

PART III

APPLICATIONS IN PRACTICE

CHAPTER 10

EDUCATIONAL APPLICATIONS

The definition of mental retardation that is presented in this manual will affect current school practices of providing special education services and, generally, will bring these practices into closer alignment with the intent of federal law. In this chapter we describe how current special education practices will be shaped by this definition of mental retardation and ask users of the manual to consider several direct implications of the definition upon current educational practices, namely:

1. Testing conducted for the purposes of making a diagnosis and developing or evaluating educational programs measures an individual student's *functioning level or ability at a given point in time, not the actual potential of that student.*

2. The diagnosis of mental retardation leads to a profile of individually defined supports, not to a specific school or educational program placement; placement and supports are not synonymous.

3. The terms used to describe a person's intensities of needed supports (intermittent, limited, extensive, and pervasive) do not replace the old labels of "educable" and "trainable" or "mild," "moderate," "severe," and "profound." Instead, these new terms correspond to specific intensities of needed supports reflecting a person's functioning within the various adaptive skill areas and their needs in three other dimensions: Psychological/Emotional Considerations, Physical/Health/Etiology Considerations, and Environmental Considerations.

4. Numerous variations in adaptive skill functioning are possible across individuals diagnosed as having mental retardation and even within a single individual over time. Individualized Educational Programs (IEPs) must reflect students' specific profiles of functioning by providing a complementary program of appropriate supports and placement in the least restrictive environment.

5. Students' needs for supports will constitute an expanded area for assessment and intervention. Supports are likely to be necessary in two or more adaptive skills areas, but also may be needed to address identified habilitation goals (psychological and emotional characteristics, health needs, and physical conditions) and to strengthen aspects of students' life environments.

6. "With appropriate supports over a sustained period, the life functioning of the person with mental retardation will generally improve." In rare cases, improvement in the life functioning of a person with mental retardation may occur without supports and may be significant enough that the label of mental retardation becomes unwarranted. For *all* students with mental retardation, some improvement in life functioning is a likely result of having the appropriate supports. Thus, because students' supports needs change with improvement and with age, their IEPs and other profiles of needed supports provided by other community agencies must be redefined regularly so they remain relevant.

CURRENT LAWS INFLUENCING
SPECIAL EDUCATION PRACTICES

Under the provisions of current laws in education and vocational rehabilitation, school services for individuals with mental retardation and pervasive needed supports can begin at birth or during the first 2 years of life. Typically, the broader label of developmental delay may be used during the preschool years and a diagnosis of mental retardation, after age 5. In most school systems, under the Individuals with Disabilities Education Act (IDEA) and state regulations, persons with mental retardation may receive special education through age 21. The mandated processes by which special education services are delivered include initial referral, assessment and identification of the disability, development of the IEP, placement in the least restrictive environment, and an annual evaluation of student progress in the program. Depending on the age of the student, various individualized programs are developed by school staff with the student, the family, and, as appropriate, relevant community service agencies. During the infant and toddler years, Individualized Family Service Plans (IFSPs) are written to address needs of the child and family. During the remainder of the preschool years and through high school or age 21, IEPs are written to guide instruction. For junior high and high school and postschool-age students with mental retardation, Individualized Transitional Programs (ITPs) complement IEPs and guide the transition from schools and education to community services and work.

Students may be harmed by an exclusive focus upon educational services or supports during their school years or supports that start and end with the school day, especially if critical psychological/emotional, health/physical, or environmental supports are omitted. One inference of the definition of mental retardation is that the identified supports be broadened beyond direct educational services. A second inference is that the recipients of some services be expanded to include the family. Most school-age children, adolescents, and young adults with mental retardation live as a member of a family or foster family. Environmental supports include services that enable the family to fulfill its many functions of child-rearing: affection; socialization; daily care, including providing for health and safety of its members, shelter, food, and clothing; economic support; recreation; and educational/vocational opportunities (A. Turnbull, Summers, and Brotherson, 1984).

Research has demonstrated that people with mental retardation who move from more restrictive institutional placements to less restrictive living options often make significant improvements in their adaptive skills (Conroy and Bradley, 1985; Conroy, Efthimiou, and Lemanowicz, 1982), in activity patterns (O'Neill, Brown, Gordon, Schonhorn, and Greer, 1981), and/or in their behavioral characteristics (Landesman-Dwyer, 1981). Yet, despite these findings, most states fail to offer families public funds to support the sometimes costly retention of children with disabilities in their natural homes. Braddock and his coworkers (Braddock, Hemp, Fujiura, Backelder, and Mitchell, 1990) reported that less than 2 percent of all tax dollars for persons with developmental disabilities is made available to these families. A supports-based definition of mental retardation infers that public agencies serving persons with mental retardation and developmental disabilities (schools and mental retardation/developmental disabilities agencies) extend their outcomes beyond enhancement of an individual's adaptive skill level during the school years to include (a) supports that counter significantly limiting factors in that person's environment and thus maximize habilitation goals related to health, physical, and psychological or functional wellness and (b) supports that foster environmental characteristics of a satisfying life (choice, competence, respect, community presence, and participation in the environment).

Diagnosis of mental retardation must be followed by the identification of supports needed in adaptive skills (education), medical/physical or psychological services, and the individual's current life environments (e.g., home, school, leisure, community, and work). Thus, being identified as having mental retardation suggests that some supports with functions matched to individual needs will facilitate development throughout life, especially at critical points in the life cycle. Because the specific needs and their intensities will change across an individual's lifespan, the importance of planning for the future cannot be overemphasized. Planning for the upcoming school transition should start during the preschool years. Transition planning will become more complex following adolescence, when the student enters the period between school and adulthood. School staff, nonschool agency staff, family members, and the student fill key roles on the planning and evaluation team discussed in the next section.

PLANNING AND EVALUATING THE EDUCATIONAL PROGRAM

DIAGNOSIS VERSUS PLACEMENT

Beyond identification of the disability of mental retardation, two important intents of the definition are to base intensities of supports on adaptive skill performance and other multidimensional considerations and to eliminate the use of severity labels to designate educational placement. Such misuse has led to questionable practices in special education classification, such as (a) rigid and at times almost automatic placement in classes by identified level of IQ; (b) the reinforcement of IQ-based and prejudicial labels (i.e., educable, trainable), which influence expectations of achievement; and (c) placement decisions made prior to the design of the IEP. Instead, the types or intensities of educational supports needed by an individual student with mental retardation is related primarily to his or her current performance on multifaceted assessments across adaptive skill areas, not to degree of mental retardation. Accurate assessment of adaptive skills will rely on considerable observations across settings, clinical judgment, a consideration of the prior intensities of supports available to an individual, and re-evaluation over time. For example, persons who have had few opportunities for an integrated life and/or little or no appropriate education may initially demonstrate extensive limitations in many adaptive skills. However, with the addition of environmental supports and effective educational programming, they may gain sufficient skills to reduce their limitations or, in rare cases, may no longer exhibit limitations in adaptive skills consistent with the definition of mental retardation.

DEVELOPMENT OF INDIVIDUALIZED PROGRAMS

IEP team responsibilities. Schools have typically focused primarily upon designing a curriculum to teach skills, sometimes relying more on a set curriculum associated with a given IQ-dependent level of "severity." Thus, a person placed in a classroom for students with moderate mental retardation traditionally may have been expected to address a set of skills associated with individuals designated as being "trainable." The definition changes the IEP team's responsibilities *from* "matching" a student having a mental retardation designation with a set school location and curriculum *to* an IEP team that:

1. Collects and analyzes a broader set of assessment information (adaptive skills and limitations; physical, medical, and psychological characteristics and needs; and environmental strengths and limitations).

2. Translates these assessment data into a profile of needed supports to compensate for, improve, or overcome the student's current performance in specific areas of weakness.

3. Develops plans (i.e., IFSPs, IEPs, ITPs) to address how the educational services and other needed supports will be delivered to the individual, involving agencies beyond the school when appropriate.

4. Designs programs that include the student, to the greatest extent possible, in educational, social, and leisure activities with peers who do not have disabilities and supplies the educational supports to enable successful inclusion and prevent segregated programs.

5. Evaluates the individual's progress under these plans and makes improvements on at least an annual basis considering assessment data, diagnosis, actual services and supports delivered, location of placement, the individual's progress, and the family's and student's degree of satisfaction.

One of the first implications evident in the Definition, Classification, and Systems of Supports is that schools will expand their assessment range to embrace a more comprehensive view of adaptive skill strengths and needs and will assess needed supports. After students are referred to the special services committee in a school system, their assessment initially will reflect the guidelines identified in chapter 4 for intellectual functioning and adaptive skills. These assessment data first are used to make a diagnosis as to whether or not a student has mental retardation. However, given that a student meets the key criteria for mental retardation, more programmatic use can be obtained from the adaptive skill data than simply a confirmation of diagnosis, *if* adaptive skill measures have been selected that provide specific information suited to educational planning (Browder, 1991).

ASSESSMENT TO YIELD PROFILES OF SUPPORT

Traditionally, assessment fills three primary purposes in schools: (a) to determine eligibility for special education services, (b) to design an educational plan by identifying current and needed skills, and (c) to evaluate instructional program outcomes. This manual adds two more purposes: (d) to identify the supports that correspond to needs in adaptive skills as well as in the medical/physical dimension, the psychological domain, and the environmental domain; and (e) to evaluate the effects of the added supports. Thus, the multidisciplinary assessment team must broaden its assessment focus to evaluate the types and intensities of supports needed to enhance a given individual's independence, productivity, and community integration.

Assessment should address both the individual's skills and limitations and the strengths and limitations of the environments used by that person (home, school, and community). Generally, the person's intensities of needed supports will parallel his or her assessed degree of limitations, but this may not always be the case. Further, the presence of various medical conditions or physical limitations, *apart* from the diagnosis of mental retardation, may contribute to the need for specific supports matched to those conditions or limitations. For example, some persons with cerebral palsy and mental retardation will need certain supports because of the cerebral palsy, such as long-term individualized programs of therapy, access to adaptive equipment, and, often, corrective surgery. Another individual with mental retardation whose limitations in adaptive skills could be minimal may require extensive, though time-limited, medical supports for heart surgery. Finally, the presence of emotional or psychological disabilities may require additional specific supports not needed by those free of such disability (e.g., increased family respite, in-home behavior management assistance, programming based on functional analyses). Table 10.1 lists some of these assessment options that provide the evaluation team with data to profile needed supports, plan appropriate programs, and evaluate their outcome. Assessment of needed supports will often require practical, informal, and criterion-referenced methods rather than formal, norm-based measures.

Once these assessments are complete, the task of IEP teams centers upon the translation of these assessment data into profiles of corresponding supports, reflecting identified strengths and limitations in adaptive skills, environments (e.g., home, school, leisure, community, and work), and students' physical or emotional characteristics as well as any relevant medical or psychological implications. The school would involve the family, the student, and, in some cases, family friends or advocates along with community and child and adult service providers in the planning process. The findings and decision-making process are shared by the school, family, and other relevant agencies. Although the school may not provide all the supports directly, referrals are used to obtain the needed supports that go beyond school services. Furthermore, when community services are provided using a case management approach that continues during and after the school years, identification and provision of needed supports should be improved.

Defining needed supports. Supports targeted during the school years, like those targeted during adulthood, will vary along a number of dimensions. First, support may not be necessary in all areas of adaptive skills; in physical, medical, or psychological services; or in all environments. Second, support requirements may be time-limited or ongoing, thus indicating the importance of repeated assessment of progress and needed supports with corresponding adjustment of supports. Third, the intensities of supports required, the types of support resources, and the support functions will be specific to the individual and the life cycle. In chapter 3 four intensities of supports were described: intermittent, limited, extensive, and pervasive (see Table 3.1).

Support resources may come to a person from four sources: (a) the individual student (e.g., skills and competencies, ability to make choices), (b) other people (e.g., family, friends, co-workers), (c) technology (e.g., assistive devices, job accommodations), and (d) habilitation services. Supports during the school years, like those in adult life,

TABLE 10.1 Types of School Assessment Relevant to Students With Mental Retardation

Assessment function	Assessment method
1. To establish priority skill and students activity needs for IEP in relevant skill domain	**Ecological inventory**: interview student, family, teachers, relevant community members, peers; observation in relevant home, school, work, leisure, and other community settings
Relevant to: Students of all ages *Frequency*: Roughly every 3 years unless student moves, then repeat following move	
2. To plan for school to work transition following graduation (ITP)[a]	**Transitional and vocational planning assessment**: interview and observation; **Alternate methods**: work sampling, income and benefits, increased integrated activities, etc.
Relevant to: Students ages 14 to 16 through school completion *Frequency*: Update annually or as needed	
3. To evaluate IEP[b] objectives	**Observation in natural settings**: Probe and training data; **Alternate methods**: family report, schedule changes, peer comments, self-assessment, etc.
Relevant to: All students *Frequency*: Roughly each week for performance data	
4. To evaluate behavioral problems and	**Functional analyses**: interviews and program development observation; **Direct observation**: mastery of replacement skills, reduction in excess behavior, increases in social interactions, etc; **Alternate methods**: interview and observation
Relevant to: Students whose behavior interferes with their health, with school and community acceptance, and/or with learning *Frequency*: Multiple times per day to less often	
5. To determine student and family satisfaction	**Satisfaction measures**: interview questionnaire, observation; **Alternate methods**: monthly pay, happiness self-report, emergency room visits and days of illness, number social activities, choices and peer contacts, etc.
Relevant to: All students *Frequency*: Annually or more often	

[a]Individualized Transitional Program. [b]Individualized Educational Program.

must not simply be viewed as being synonymous with direct educational (or other habilitation) services. For example, supports that come from the individual are encouraged because they are adaptive and more reliable and normalized, though the related skills to provide self-support initially may need to be taught and supplemental supports from other sources may also be required.

Support functions. A review of the seven support functions applied to school-age persons and their rules for use will make the case study applications presented next in this chapter more meaningful. *Integration is a primary means for reducing functional disabilities, whereas the purpose of support is to advance and enrich the success of integration.* Thus, natural, less intrusive supports that are still effective are preferred over artificial supports that may be less reliable or stigmatizing. Depending on the individual student and area(s) of need, supports may be ongoing throughout the school years or may vary in intensity and presence during preschool, elementary, middle or high school years, and postschool years. Finally, if supports appear to be less needed or not needed and are reduced or withdrawn, schools must monitor the effects of these reductions on the person's functioning in everyday life. This last rule has special significance as a student transfers from one educational system to another by simply moving or by growing older (infant education to preschool to elementary school, etc.) or transitions from the schools to adult services and vocational rehabilitation. At these times, due to changing school and service regulations and program staff, inappropriate changes in support may occur. When transitional planning incorporates the students, family members, the sending program, and the receiving program, *and* occurs *prior* to the transition, the problems resulting from unplanned modifications in supports will be minimized.

Supports provided to students with mental retardation may be categorized by their function. The seven functions (befriending, financial planning, employee assistance, behavioral support, in-home living assistance, community access and use, and health assistance) and representative example activities are listed in Table 9.1. They may be modified somewhat to accommodate persons of varying ages.

These dimensions of support will be applied next to four students with mental retardation or developmental delay whose ages range from 9 months to 18 years and whose specific needs for supports in education and other areas differ widely.

CASE STUDIES

High school student with limitations. First, consider a teenager with mental retardation who has limitations in several areas of adaptive skills and who is approaching graduation from secondary school:

Alice, age 18, is close to the completion of vocational training and high school graduation. Due to her strengths in social, vocational, and daily living skills, she may need only intermittent job support from the postschool special education program. Alice has spent much of her secondary school career in classes with peers who do not have limitations but has received resource teacher support to individualize her academic programs through the elementary and middle-school years and community-based training to learn community and vocational skills during her years in secondary school. Soon Alice will need medical intervention (short-term, intensive) because of a progressive visual loss that, if not treated, will end in partial sightedness, the possible termination of her current job, and an increased ongoing need for new supports in other areas. Alice appears to need an intermittent intensity of temporary support environmentally due to the fact that her parents are both in their late 70s and in poor health, and she currently lives at home. Such support will enable her and her parents to engage in financial planning and will assist her to choose a place to live in her community and to learn to live with limited supports, depending on her success and choices. A profile of Alice's needed supports is given in Table 10.2.

Upper elementary-age student with limitations and behavior problems.
Jared is a 10-year-old boy whose typical behavior has been described by some as being "autistic-like" and is characterized as including stereotypic movements of the hands and body; infrequent smiling, laughing, or affection towards others; and no communication except several signs for activities and for "more" and frequent instances of showing people what he desires. Jared does not initiate performance of routine self-care tasks without prompting and reminders. When asked to sit at a table and work on "prevocational" tasks involving paper or sorting or to perform other tasks he does not like, Jared typically refuses by running away from the task and/or engaging in tantrum behavior. He has been attending a regional self-contained classroom for students with mental retardation in a separate school since he was 5 years old, despite the fact that he must ride a bus for one hour both ways. As a 4-year-old, he attended a local church preschool and fit in fairly well. His two brothers and one sister attend public school near their home.

When his siblings and parents were asked to identify Jared's friends, they listed themselves, other relatives, two neighborhood children who visit them, and Jared's doctor, dentist, babysitter, teacher, and speech therapist. Jared's family typically avoid extended trips into the community with him because of his tantrum behavior; his mother thinks he is afraid of the noises and commotion present in grocery stores and at the mall. However, the family does enjoy hiking and swimming together throughout the year in the city recreation center and in parks.

Jared's family members worry about his future and wish that he would be included in the middle school program with the support of a special education teacher and communication therapist. They are eager to have him attend school with his siblings, his neighbors, and his peers because they have noted favorable changes in Jared's behavior when he is with peers rather than others who have severe disabilities. Recently, teachers have reduced his tantrum behavior in stores by equipping him with a portable headset radio. Although his parents also have been encouraged by his acquisition of some practical skills when taught in community settings (e.g., purchasing a snack, crossing streets with assistance), they still worry about his absence of friends, his poor social skills and behavior problems in school, the predominance of school time spent in a segregated setting, and his long bus rides to and from school. His family knows that he has only 11 years left in his schooling and wonder whether supported employment will be an option for him, given his behavior problems at school and in public as well as the poor employment record of recent graduates of the regional school.

TABLE 10.2 Current Supports Needed by Alice

Dimension/Area	Support function	Activities	Time	Intensity
I. Intellectual Functioning and Adaptive Skills				
Work	Community access	To and from work	Ongoing	Limited
	Employee assistance	Job tasks	Ongoing	Intermittent
	Befriending	Learning interdependence with co-workers, supervisors	Ongoing	Intermittent
Home living	Teaching	Housekeeping	Ongoing	Intermittent
		Food management	Ongoing	Intermittent
	Budgeting	Budgeting	Ongoing	Intermittent
Community use/ Social skills	Community access Befriending/teaching	Leisure activities with peers, co-workers	Ongoing	Intermittent
Functional academics	Financial planning	Adjusting work benefits	Ongoing	Intermittent
II. Psychological / Emotional Considerations[a]				
III. Physical/Health/ Etiology Considerations	Health assistance	Eye surgery	Time limited	Extensive
IV. Environmental Considerations	Befriending	Options and choice of home, circle of friends	Time limited	Intermittent
	Financial planning	Budgeting, advocating for benefits	Ongoing	Limited

[a]None for this client.

121

Because a major purpose of supports is to enhance the success of integration and reduce functional limitations, Jared and his family demonstrate extensive needed supports. For the past year, his parents have been active members of the local school's special education advisory committee. Although still incomplete, plans are being made to return Jared and several of his classmates to their own school system; several teachers and paraprofessionals will be hired to assist in this process of starting a local program to serve Jared's needs.

The middle-school principal and staff are also involved in this planning because the local school program will be started first with three students of middle-school age, who now all attend the regional program. His current teacher will move with these three students, initiating some community-based teaching along with shared teaching in integrated activities: home room, art, chorus, cafeteria use, physical education, library, and assemblies.

The school system will seek assistance from the state Department of Education to provide a *functional analysis* of Jared's behavior problems and their possible relation to his lack of effective communication. This information will be employed to design a skill-building program that matches the apparent escape communication function of his behavior problems; current programs that rely mainly on timeout and response cost will be phased out. Several of Jared's and his family's areas of needed support are outlined in Table 10.3.

Preschooler with extensive needed supports. Third, consider Jake, who is 4 years old and has been receiving special education services since birth. Jake has mental retardation and cerebral palsy, does not speak, and, because of his movement limitations, is dependent upon others for many of his daily activities. For the past year he has attended a private Montessori preschool primarily serving children without limitations. Jake has received daily therapy during typical routine activities under the regular supervision of the local public school division's itinerant communication, occupational, and physical therapists. With their assistance and that of the local school division's early childhood special education teacher, who provides consultation to the private preschool teachers on Jake's behalf, his teachers and parents have applied the principle of partial participation and taught him to perform parts of, and to assist in, most routine tasks and leisure activities. They have developed ways to teach Jake to communicate his preferences and to indicate when he wants routine and play activities started and stopped, and they have utilized electronic switches for him to control many activities.

As a result of Jake's inclusion in an integrated preschool, he has frequent opportunities during and after school to interact with peers who do not have limitations and can express personal pleasures and dislikes, nonsymbolically make many choices daily, assist in most routines by initiating and performing some of the core steps, and is included in numerous social activities with peers.

His mother, who has recently returned to work to supplement the family income, needs reliable after-school child care for Jake and his 7-year-old sister. The local after-school program will not accept Jake until he is 5 years old. In the meantime, the local community services agency will train an in-home care provider to watch the children

TABLE 10.3 Supports Needed by Jared and His Family

Dimension/Area	Support function	Activities	Time	Intensity
I. Intellectual Functioning and Adaptive Skills				
Social skills	Behavioral support	Functional assessment	Ongoing	Extensive
	Befriending	Design and implementation of effective nonaversive skill-building program with choice-making	Ongoing	Pervasive
		Social interactions with peers in 5th grade	Ongoing	Extensive
Leisure	Teaching	Ecological inventory	Ongoing	Extensive
	Befriending	Embed in friendship after school and 6th grade activities	Ongoing	Extensive
	Community use			
Communication	Teaching	Investigate facilitated communication	Ongoing	Extensive
		Create communication systems	Ongoing	Extensive
		Teach across daily routines	Ongoing	Extensive
Functional academics	Teaching	Ecological inventory	Ongoing	Extensive
		Embed in adapted 6th grade activities	Ongoing	Extensive
Home living	Teaching	Ecological inventory	Ongoing	Extensive
		Apply functional skills (social behavior, functional academics, etc.)	Ongoing	Extensive

continued

TABLE 10.3 (continued)

Dimension/Area		Support function	Activities	Time	Intensity
I. Intellectual/ Adaptive Skills					
	Health & safety	Teaching	Ecological inventory	Ongoing	Extensive
		Health assistance	Embed in adapted 6th grade and alternate community based instruction	Ongoing	Extensive
	Work	Teaching	Job sampling in school-based jobs	Ongoing	Extensive
			Advocating and planning for school reform	Ongoing	Extensive
II. Psychological/ Emotional Considerations		Behavioral support	Functional assessment	Ongoing	Pervasive
			Design multi-component nonaversive intervention	Ongoing	Pervasive
			Teach family members	Time limited	Extensive
			Consider psycho-pharmacological therapy	Time limited	Intermittent
			Respite staff assistance in home	Time limited	Intermittent
III. Physical/Health/ Etiology Considerations[a]					
IV. Environmental Considerations		Community/school access	Advocating and planning for inclusion in middle and high school	Ongoing	Extensive

[a]None for this client.

124

after school. Jake's parents, teachers, and speech therapist want to expand his expressive skills with an augmentative communication system and will seek assessment and training advice through the school and private consultation. Assessment by his IEP team indicated several types and areas of needed supports for Jake and his family (Table 10.4).

Jake's family and teachers recognize the changing needs for supports over time as he moves into the public school and is included with his peers in kindergarten, as his parents have requested. Jake's classroom teachers will continue to need time and support from special education teachers in order to identify and evaluate IEP objectives and adapt class activities to meet his needs. His related service needs will continue in communication and physical and occupational therapy. Furthermore, as Jake grows older, orthopedic surgery may be needed, and new adaptive equipment will be necessary to promote improved positioning and movement and to reduce his dependence on others; vocational assessment and job adaptation will be required in his early teen years in order to enable him to obtain employment.

An infant at risk for mental retardation. Lauren is 9-months-old and was born to a 17-year-old unmarried mother who used drugs and alcohol during her pregnancy. Lauren has delays in all areas of development, though these delays were minimized because her mother entered drug treatment during the last 3 months of pregnancy and has remained off drugs. Lauren is functioning developmentally about 3 to 5 months behind schedule. There have been clear improvements in her attentiveness to events and people, her social behavior and responsivity to others, and her ability to calm herself and to be comforted by others.

Since Lauren's birth, educational programming has been available to Lauren, her mother, and her grandmother, who cares for her when the mother is working or completing high school requirements. A public school teacher specializing in infants visits the home twice weekly and works directly with Lauren as she plays with her mother and grandmother. In addition, the teacher has worked with the mother, the grandmother, and a caseworker from social services to design an IFSP, which specifies objectives, supports, and services for Lauren and her family. Table 10.5 lists some of these areas and functions of support.

The teacher and caseworker have reduced the family's confusion over obtaining services and supports and helping them plan for Lauren's future. Her adaptive skill objectives address needed developmental skills. While working directly with Lauren, the teacher also instructs the mother and grandmother as she models simple facilitative methods designed to motivate Lauren to improve and use targeted skills during natural daily routines. Other objectives for the mother and grandmother have focused upon Lauren's fussiness and her restricted attention span. The teacher, along with the public health nurse, has intervened by giving the mother and grandmother techniques to adjust Lauren's sleep and wake schedule, encourage self-comfort, "read" Lauren's cues so they can respond appropriately to her fussiness and inattention, improve their nurturing of Lauren, and identify and offer preferred activities.

Dimension/Area	Support function	Activities	Time	Intensity
I. Intellectual Functioning and Adaptive Skills				
Social skills, leisure Communication	Befriending	Interaction with peers	Ongoing	Limited
	Health assistance	Selection of communication device	Time limited	Extensive
Functional academics	Teaching	Instruction to use	Ongoing	Extensive
	Teaching	Ecological inventory	Ongoing	Intermittent
		Embed in adapted preschool lessons/activities	Ongoing	Extensive
Home living	Health assistance	Material adaptations and switches	Ongoing	Limited
	Teaching	Use of switches and communication device	Ongoing	Limited
	Teaching	Participation in home living routines	Ongoing	Extensive
Self-care	Health assistance	Participation in self-care routines	Ongoing	Extensive
II. Psychological/Emotional Considerations[a]				
III. Physical/Health/ Etiology Considerations	Health assistance	Physical therapy and related activities	Ongoing	Extensive
IV. Environmental Considerations	Community/school access	Parents join support and advocate groups to prepare community for integration	Ongoing	Extensive
	Befriending	Respite care and after-school care routines	Ongoing	Extensive
		Planning for placement in kindergarten	Time limited	Extensive

[a]None for this client.

126

TABLE 10.5 Supports Needed by Lauren and Her Family

Dimension/Area	Support function	Activities	Time	Intensity
I. Intellectual Functioning and Adaptive Skills	Teaching (Lauren)	Routine-based facilitative techniques to teach development and self-calming (teacher & public health nurse)	Ongoing	Extensive
	Teaching (mother & grandmother)	Methods to "read" infant's cues, schedule and activity adjustment nurturing (teacher & nurse)	Ongoing	Extensive
II. Psychological/Emotional Considerations	Behavioral support (mother)	Continue free enrollment in drug treatment and support group program	Time limited	Extensive
III. Physical/Health/Etiology Considerations	Health assistance (Lauren)	Regular developmental checks as follow up for prenatal drug at hospital clinic	Ongoing	Limited
		Home visits from nurse	Ongoing	Limited
IV. Environmental Considerations	Employee assistance (mother)	Complete high school equivalency test	Time limited	Extensive
		Use job counseling to improve employment	Biweekly	Extensive

continued

TABLE 10.5 (continued)

Dimension/Area	Support function	Activities	Time	Intensity
	Financial planning caseworker)	Apply for Aid to Dependent Children	Time limited	Limited
		Apply for Medicaid	Time limited	Limited
		Apply to WIC (Womens, Infants, and Children) for nutritional information, formula, milk	Time limited	Limited
	Community access and use	Transportation program to high school, clinic, drug support	Biweekly	Extensive
	Home living	Support in feeding, sleeping, and calming methods from public health nurse	Biweekly	Extensive

In all four cases, Alice, Jared, Jake, and Lauren, the revised tasks of the educational team include more data-based future planning, a job that is particularly difficult for families, but one that is consistent with transition planning to facilitate progress throughout life. The definition of mental retardation provided in this manual requires that schools and families coordinate with others on the assessment and provision of supports. For families, advocacy often follows future planning activities, whereas schools will be engaged in program planning and improvement. As A. Turnbull (1988) noted, perhaps two thirds of the transition planning skills used by family members are generic across different life stages, with the remainder being specific to the particular transition in question.

CURRICULUM DEVELOPMENT AND INSTRUCTIONAL IMPLICATIONS

IEP DEVELOPMENT

As illustrated in all four case studies, the school curricula for students identified as having mental retardation must be individually defined if they are to result in meaningful outcomes. Because most students with mental retardation are unable to learn as quickly or retain and generalize learned skills as well as their typical peers, it becomes essential to individualize their curriculum and, in terms of PL 94-142, to provide "specially designed instruction." However, specially designed or individualized instruction is *not* synonymous with placement in a specialized class or school. Intensity of services and location of service delivery should not be made interdependent (Taylor, 1988). Current research on segregated school programs has emphasized the undesirable side effects of equating special education with educational programs separate from peers without disabilities (Gartner and Lipsky, 1987; Snell and Eichner, 1989). School programs that are *not individualized* to reflect student needs can evolve into repetitive or "watered down" versions of the regular academic curriculum or may rigidly focus on a fixed sequence of developmental milestones with no adaptation to the student's chronological age or functional needs. These approaches typically have meant that students do not attain skill outcomes that are functional for them (Gartner and Lipsky, 1987).

Assessment for the purpose of devising an effective, individualized, educational program is, by necessity, informal, ongoing, and multifaceted and involves the collection and analysis of many types of data from many sources (Table 10.1). Assessment methods include: (a) interaction with the student during familiar activities; (b) direct observation of the student's behavior during activities identified as having practical value to the student; (c) interviews with care providers, teachers, peers, employers, the student, and others having information relevant to the student's current abilities or future needs; (d) interviews and observation to assess a student's activity preferences and choice-making ability; and (e) alternate techniques to assess progress, for example, percentage of IEP objectives accomplished annually or changes in the number of behavior problems classified by intensity (Meyer and Evans, 1989) and lifestyle outcomes, for example, social integration measured by the amount of school time spent in activities with peers who do not have disabilities (Bellamy, Newton, LeBaron, and Horner, 1990; Kennedy, Horner, Newton, and Kanda, 1990).

Typically, standardized tasks and norms are not employed in these types of assessment. Informal assessments are devised by teachers and others and use standards that reflect the student's chronological age and the local community (Horner, Sprague, and Flannery, 1990). The resulting curriculum should match the student's current chronological age and reflect activities, criteria, and demands of the local community/or culture in which the individual resides. The range of assessment data collected depends on the purpose but may be broad and should address daily and predicted future life functions: domestic or personal management and leisure and social, community, and vocational areas.

Teachers must work with many others in order to collect meaningful assessment data, including parents and family members, the individual student, peers, related services staff (occupational, physical, communication, and recreation therapists), school psychologist, and school and family health personnel. When data are collected, shared, and genuinely used by the educational team, the process is likely to be both more efficient and more accurate. Assessment procedures are developed that are tailored to examine aspects of school, home, and community life pertinent to the student's daily and future life (Browder, 1991).

In the first area of assessment, the teacher (with others on the IEP team) administers an *ecological inventory* or an *environmental assessment* to identify a pool of skills and activities considered important for a student across domains of life skill (e.g., Ford et al., 1989; Helmstetter, 1989; Neel and Billingsley, 1989). Parents, teachers (current and future), and others who have knowledge about future community services or employment will be asked, usually in an interview, several questions to generate a pool of potential skills. Questions 4-10 are asked to assess priority activities and to help differentiate more needed activities from those that are less needed.

1. What skill clusters or activities does the person need to function in the environment in the same way as do their same age peers (e.g., in home, school, leisure, community, work)?

2. What skill clusters or activities will the person need to learn in the near future to function like peers in targeted environments (e.g., home, school, leisure, community, work)?

3. What skill clusters or activities, either present or needed by the student, are highly preferred by the student?

4. Which of these skill clusters are critical, essential, or of high priority to this student (or family) in the domestic, personal management, leisure, community, and vocational domains? (more needed activity/skills)

5. Which of these skill clusters, if any, are critical to the student's health and safety? (more needed activity/skills)

6. Which of these activities are highly preferred by the student? (more needed activity/skills)

7. Which activities will promote increased independence and interdependence in integrated community settings? (more needed activities/skills)

8. Which activities will contribute to the student's happiness, acceptance by others, and personal life satisfaction? (more needed activities/skills)

9. Which activities either cannot be taught or can only be taught with great difficulty (performed very infrequently, require great travel, necessitate simulation to teach)? (less easily taught activities/skills)

10. Which activities (a) are or will be *age inappropriate*, or (b) are highly time-limited (not valuable beyond the student's near future), or (c) have questionable future value? (less needed activities/skills)

Conferring with the family and school staff, teachers draft a set of high priority skills or activities representing all areas of relevance to the student. These data and other assessment information are shared at the IEP meeting. During this meeting, educational staff and parents (and, when appropriate, the student) focus on four major tasks:

- Review of formal evaluation and current levels of performance
- Development of goals and objectives
- Determination of placement
- Determination of related services

Beyond these tasks, there are many preparation activities that precede the IEP meeting and include the family, and there are initial meeting steps and closing procedures (A. Turnbull and Turnbull, 1990).

IMPROVED APPROACHES TO TEACHING AND LEARNING

The definition of mental retardation in this manual emphasizes the value and critical impact of integration upon the life of individuals with mental retardation. Teaching methods should be socially valid and promote generalized skill use in normalized environments used by the student: home, school, leisure, community, and work. "Best practices" indicate that when skills are taught as integrated parts of functional routines, rather than in isolation, students with mental retardation demonstrate better skill generalization and retention. Rather than simply scheduled for instruction in discrete blocks of time, basic motor, language, and social skills are taught as they occur or are needed, naturally *embedded* within routine activities. This principle of integrated instruction applies as well to the provision of related services by occupational, physical, communication, and recreation therapists (Giangreco, York, and Rainforth, 1989). Because peers without mental retardation can serve as powerful models for language, behavior, dress, and social skills, schooling alongside peers enables planned and sponta-neous peer-to-peer instruction not typically possible in separate schools and classrooms where all students have disabilities. Finally, educational approaches for addressing behavior problems, whether mild or serious, are characterized by (a) assessment of the function or purpose that such behavior serves for the student and (b) nonaversive interventions that employ short-term strategies (e.g., environmental changes; provision of new, immediate consequences) and long-term educational strategies and program improvement (e.g., teaching alternate adaptive responses that match the function of a behavior problem, increasing opportunities for integration).

There are many barriers to the successful inclusion of students with mental retardation in school programs. These barriers are not limited to teacher "know how" or to negative attitudes. A strong argument has been made that current school organization discourages teacher collaboration and problem-solving and encourages teacher specialization, categorization of students with and without disabilities, and standardization of school products and services (Skrtic, 1991). Furthermore, Skrtic argued that schools operate like "machine bureaucracies" in that they are led more by following a manual of rules and regulations than by following an educational leader. School administrators try to balance the precarious load of a machine bureaucracy for operating schools and a professional bureaucracy for organizing curriculum, students, and teaching staff, but inclusive programs fit poorly within either organization.

Traditional special education programs are viewed as being "decoupled" from the rest of the school system, as separate and often independent educational systems with little or no linkage to regular education (Gartner and Lipsky, 1987). In response, some professionals have called for a reorganization and restructuring of school systems, not only within school administration but between teachers and programs in individual schools (Lipsky and Gartner, 1991; Skrtic, 1991). Yet, the debate on restructuring schools to merge special education with regular education is still very lively, and consensus has not been reached among special educators (Lloyd, Singh, and Repp, 1991). The emergence of school-based management, in which principals and their staffs are given more autonomy from the central administration for shaping an individual school program that serves *all* students in the school, has been identified as a movement that is conducive to the successful inclusion of students with disabilities in regular education. However, other school characteristics will also need to be reformed if special education is to become part of regular education and if students who have special need labels are to be meaningfully included with their peers who do not (e.g., more collaboration among educators on students who have special learning needs; problem-solving to invent new solutions and programs rather than a focus on the perfection of standard programs) (Skrtic, 1991).

Adaptations in instruction and curriculum must be made in order to include students with mental retardation successfully in regular classes with their peers (Nevin and Thousand, 1987). The success of these adaptations ultimately depends further upon collaborative teamwork to plan and enact these school changes (Graden and Bauer, 1992; York and Vandercook, 1990). Collaborative teams can include IEP teams, building-based planning teams, planning teams organized around specific students, and collaborative teaching teams between regular and special educators. Ironically, both areas identified as being keys to the success of school integration—*curriculum adaptation* and *collaborative teamwork*—are most in need of further empirical development and study (Giangreco and Putnam, 1991) and are often omitted from programs to prepare school administrators or teachers (Baumgart and Ferguson, 1991).

Curriculum and instructional adaptation encompass creative modifications in many aspects of planning: scheduling, grouping, class selection and enrollment, support (e.g., materials, peer, staff), integration of instruction in place of "pull out" instruction or therapy, embedding IEP objectives within regular class and school activities, the expansion of *community-based instruction* (i.e., applied teaching of functional skills in community settings) to students without disabilities and modified staffing strategies involving related services personnel, paraprofessionals, resource consultants, and teams of regular and special education teachers (Fuchs and Fuchs, 1989; Huefner, 1988; Peck, Killen, and Baumgart, 1989; Snell and Brown, in press).

Depending on students' ages, IEPs, and abilities in adaptive skills, different school activities with peers will be appropriately selected and adapted. During preschool and early elementary grades, full inclusion in regular classes will be much more frequent, but curricular adaptations are still needed to prevent a "mismatch" between the skill level of a student and the content of the lesson and to facilitate student success in mastering the relevant skills (Giangreco and Putnam, 1991; Sailor et al., 1989). The older the student with mental retardation, the more the teaching focus will be upon the development of job skills, functional academics, and independent living abilities, thus making enrollment with high-school peers in vocational courses more appropriate than with those in college preparation coursework. Individualized instruction away from the peer group context also can be appropriate for students with mental retardation both in school and community settings that are identified as being useful to the student. Two terms summarize successful curriculum planning and adaptation: individualization and support.

MODIFICATION OF PLACEMENT AND RELATED SUPPORTS

This manual does not specify levels of disability. In the recent past, respective levels were often automatically translated into service delivery systems, placements, or curricula. The practice in many school systems was to select placement contingent upon diagnosis. Often a given placement dictated not only the school a student attended but the general curriculum, which in turn dictated, to a large extent, goals and objectives. When placement procedures follow this pattern, programs are far less likely to relate to an individual's specific needs in adaptive skills or environmental and health/medical supports. Furthermore, "label specific" placements have been associated with certain outcomes: (a) they have not allowed students to attend their *home school* (the one they would have attended had they not been identified as having special needs); (b) because of separate classrooms or schools and segregated work and leisure settings, they have reduced or eliminated interactions with peers who do not have limitations; and (c) they have negatively affected the acquisition of social skills and the development of meaningful relationships and social networks among peers (Gartner and Lipsky, 1987; Sailor et al., 1989; Snell, 1991).

Stated in simple terms, federal regulations require that students with limitations receive their education to the greatest extent possible alongside their age mates without limitations and "that any move away from the regular educational setting occur only when it is not possible for that student's program, as supplemented with aids and services, to provide him or her with an appropriate education" (Snell and Eichner, 1989, p. 110). A growing body of research has demonstrated many problems with separate school and class placements, including a failure to return to mainstream, increased stigma, a lack of peer social networks, and inadequacy of learning (Gartner and Lipsky, 1987; Laski, 1991; McDonnell and Hardman, 1989). Despite these findings and the legal and logical basis for integration of students with mental retardation, current placement practices are widely divergent from school system to school system, with a predominance of separate class and school placements for students identified as having mental retardation (Danielson and Bellamy, 1989; Polloway, Epstein, Patton, Cullinon, and Luebke, 1986; U.S. Department of Education, 1988).

On an annual basis, the IEP team has the legal responsibility of changing a student's placement (and modifying their educational program) if it can show that such change is better suited to the student. At the same time, the family can request a placement change if it feels the current placement is inappropriate. Consistent with current regulations in special education and the definition's emphasis on assessment of needed supports, IEP teams can exercise their authority to request that schools support students with mental retardation so that they are included, to the greatest extent possible, alongside their peers who do not have disabilities. Such supports might be administrative, school-based, or pertain more directly to a teacher or peers. For example, administrative supports might include (a) temporary consultant help from inside or outside the system; (b) a request for waivers to state requirements for special class assignment, allowing more flexibility in scheduling and more heterogeneous groupings of students with special needs; (c) inservice training on cooperative teaching approaches or collaborative team teaching; (d) the provision of instructional aides in the regular classroom; and (e) the redistribution of regional resources (e.g., related services staff, entitlements programs for economically deprived students, instructional materials, and assistants) (Villa and Thousand, 1990).

School-based support can come from an "in-house" team of school staff members working with the principal and parents (a) to address inclusion issues around individual students; (b) to arrange schedules so integration occurs in all school activities, including academics; and (c) to adjust teaching staff assignments. Such support allows special education teachers to plan and co-teach with regular education teachers and thereby assist in the individualization of programs for students with identified special needs and with others experiencing learning needs but who have not been labeled (Ford, Davern, and Schnorr, 1992). Teacher-to-teacher support often results from sharing of talents, materials, ideas, and classroom activities and leads to effective problem solving, functional adaptation of academic subjects, and the identification of integrated contexts for teaching a variety of functional skills. Finally, peer support has been shown to be perhaps the most powerful of all supports in building meaningful relationships, promoting advocacy and respect for diversity, and enabling students with disabilities to have age-appropriate models, learn to cope with stress, and achieve positive psychosocial adjustment (Forest, 1991; Peck, Donaldson, and Pezzoli, 1990; Strully and Strully, 1985; Vandercook, York, and Forest, 1989). The use of teacher-to-teacher and peer supports appear to be more probable when the principal and staff create an atmosphere of believing that all students can learn and are valued and that supports will be given to help staff accomplish these ends.

In summary, in this chapter we have described the implications that the 1992 AAMR definition of mental retardation has for schools and public education. Briefly, the definition will influence typical practices in assessment, IEP development, placement, provision of support services, and integration of students with and without mental retardation. These influences should ultimately benefit all students, including students with mental retardation and their families.

CHAPTER 11

ADULT SERVICES APPLICATIONS

This chapter provides an overview of the impact of the 1992 definition of mental retardation on services for adults with mental retardation and the families, caregivers, service providers, and delivery systems that address their needs. The definition—with its increased specification of adaptive skills, the primacy of the environment, and focus on individual supports—has significant implications and challenges for service delivery systems for adults.

TRENDS IN SERVICE DELIVERY TO ADULTS

The four assumptions essential to the application of the definition mirror significant trends in the field of mental retardation and a growing body of knowledge that is transforming our vision of what constitutes the life possibilities for people with mental retardation. These trends include emphases on strengths and capabilities (Mount, 1987; O'Brien and Lyle, 1987), the importance of normalized or typical environments (Fiorelli and Thurman, 1979; O'Brien, 1980; Wolfensberger, 1972), the provision of age-appropriate services (Knoll and Ford, 1987; Wehman, Schleien, and Kiernan, 1980), individualized needs for supports (Perske, 1988; Smull and Bellamy, 1991), the possibilities for enhancing adaptive functioning (Conroy and Bradley, 1985), and empowerment (McFadden and Burke, 1991; Martinez, 1990).

THE PARADIGM SHIFT

These trends have coalesced into a fundamental paradigm shift and a redefinition of services to a functional supports model (Bradley and Knoll, 1990). Although much of the evolution toward a supports model has been proactive, other more negative conditions, what Smull (1989) described as a "crisis in the community," have contributed to this developing orientation of reliance on individualized supports. Many states find themselves with long waiting lists, high staff turnover, high costs, and diminishing resources. As community service systems have evolved, they have, until recently, emphasized the role of paid staff and services and de-emphasized the role of existing and natural supports. These circumstances combined to produce a crisis of both scarcity and quality.

The new paradigm is a third phase in the evolution of services for individuals with mental retardation. Preceded by the first phase of institutionalization and segregation, and, most recently (1976–1986), deinstitutionalization and community development (Bradley and Knoll, 1990), this new era of community membership demands a redefinition of services.

Most existing community services are structured with two implicit conceptions: the notion of individual deficits and a continuum of services. The deficits of an individual with mental retardation were to be addressed by services that provided training to overcome these deficits, preparing the individual to move further on the continuum of services. Inherent in the conceptualization of this continuum is the idea that services are arranged in serial fashion, designed to afford greater degrees of independence when the individual had mastered certain skills. The continuum assumed that the individual would "progress" along the continuum, moving from service to service. Service continua have been described for children in terms of education and for adults in terms of living arrangements and day/vocational services (Taylor, 1988). For the concept of the residential continuum, progress was equated with moving from living arrangement to living arrangement (e.g., residential facility to group home to supervised apartment), diminishing the possibilities for stability in people's lives. Individuals were to fit into services, and when they no longer did, whether due to progress or regression, they moved on.

The conceptualization of the service continuum derives from the principle of the least restrictive environment, which has shaped service development for people with disabilities for the past 20 years (Taylor, 1988). Services provided in the settings on the more restrictive end of the continuum were perceived as being more intensive than those services provided in the less restrictive, opposite end. Intense needs for service were perceived as being addressed in more restrictive, typically segregated settings.

SHIFTS INHERENT IN THE DEFINITION

The view represented by the definition in this manual emphasizes attitudes and practices that recognize the full citizenship of people with mental retardation while recognizing that mental retardation constitutes a significant limitation. The increased specification of adaptive skills in the definition is the source of many of the shifts in thinking and affirmations of emergent thinking in service delivery, particularly to adults (see chapter 4). Community environments as the context for the measurement and expression of adaptive skills assume a primacy, not as a particular model for service delivery, but rather as the environment for all people. This affirmation of community as the naturally occurring environment of individuals with mental retardation also serves to recognize and affirm the family as the most basic, natural environment. Supports to families follow logically and simply from this conceptualization.

The definitional focus on individual needs guides service delivery toward individual planning and functional supports and away from program models to which individual needs are to be subsumed. The focus on the intensities of individual needed supports interrupts the pattern, common to most service delivery systems, of equating intensities of service needs with restrictiveness of setting or of being synonymous with any a priori choice of settings.

The search for "community environments typical of the individuals's age peers" establishes full adult status for individuals with mental retardation and argues for full inclusion and participation in community life. The definition, by recognizing that limitations in some adaptive skill areas may be juxtaposed with strengths in other areas, highlights the capacities and capabilities of individuals with mental retardation. The move from the historical conception of mental retardation as representing global deficits allows the perception of people with mental retardation as *people* first and dictates intervention strategies that are targeted and functional. These juxtapositions also serve as a continual reminder of the heterogeneity of the group of people labeled as having mental retardation and the lack of predictive validity limitations in attempting to generalize about a particular person's skill levels or ceilings of abilities.

In looking at the impact of the definition on adult services, we very quickly become caught in a verbal bind: Our language has not yet fully caught up with our world view. We speak of adult services, reflecting the ways that most state and provider agencies are organized to address the needs of people with mental retardation. The definition redirects the focus of individual needs towards supports. Services can be reconceptualized as a subset of supports. They can be seen as a type of support to be provided when natural supports need supplementation, have been exhausted, are not available, or are not age or developmentally appropriate.

The process of establishing the diagnosis of mental retardation will place greater reliance on the assessment of adaptive skills, as described in chapters 3 and 4. This shift in assessment practices, both in the process of assessment and the type of information generated, is one of the major changes created by the definition.

IMPLEMENTATION ISSUES ENGENDERED BY THE DEFINITION

CURRENT VARIATION AMONG THE STATES

The implementation of this definition by state systems will likely differ, reflecting the existing variability among the states in the delivery of services and options for people with mental retardation (Lowitzer, Utley, and Baumeister, 1987). The variations among states include:

- Their rate of spending for community services (Braddock, Hemp, Fujiura, Bachelder, and Mitchell, 1990)
- The extent and structure of the Intermediate Care Facility for the Mentally Retarded (ICF/MR) program in the state, including the proportion between institutional beds and the use of community waivers
- The systems and structures in place for the delivery of community services
- Their respective mandates to serve people with mental retardation exclusively or a broader group of individuals described as having developmental disabilities

For state systems operating under the broader developmental disabilities rubric, there is further variation in whether the state has simply added developmental disabilities to its existing mental retardation mandate or whether the state has shifted to a more encompassing functional definition.

ELIGIBILITY FOR SERVICES

Service delivery programs as well as entitlement programs establish criteria for eligibility for services. State mental retardation systems utilize the definition of mental retardation as the basis for determining eligibility for state services, whether provided directly by the state or under contractual arrangement with provider agencies. In some cases state systems actually conduct individual evaluations and assessments to determine eligibility; in other cases the state system reviews documents and assessments conducted by outside professionals. In some states the criteria for the determination is established in legislation; in others, in administrative regulations that operationalize the intent of legislation. States will need to amend their eligibility criteria to incorporate the new definition.

The diagnosis of mental retardation depends on decisions reached in Dimension I (Intellectual Functioning and Adaptive Skills) of the Definition, Classification, and Systems of Supports and on the chronological age criteria. The increased specificity of adaptive skills in establishing the diagnosis of mental retardation will serve to move states away from the heavier weighting of the measure of intellectual functioning (i.e., IQ) in the intake or eligibility process. In part, the overreliance on IQ appears to be an artifact of the quantified measures available to assess IQ and the more limited array of adaptive skill measurements that yield a simplified and seemingly comparable statistic. Within bureaucracies there appears to be a tendency to reduce decision-making toward the more quantifiable, simple result. The dynamic of the multidimensional classification system and the multiple decisions required should serve as a counter-vailing force to these reductionistic tendencies.

The emphasis on adaptive skills in the diagnosis of mental retardation and the increased reliance on clinical judgment and decision-making will require access to professional expertise in the eligibility determination process. The education of professionals entering the field of mental retardation and the provision of continuing education opportunities for professionals already in the field may be required, particularly in view of the developing body of knowledge on adaptive skills.

Some delivery systems, in response to professional concerns or in some instances litigation over eligibility for services decisions, may seek to quantify the elements or, at minimum, develop standards for determinations of degree of intensities of supports. Any such efforts should not lose the focus of individual clinical assessment that is central to the definition. It is this individual focus and the process of clinical decision-making that makes it possible to address environmental considerations and the development of appropriate supports for individuals and their family. Although needs for supports are referenced in terms of age peers, the definition is structured to address the individual's abilities and needs, not group considerations.

The process of determining eligibility for services will, under the new definition, focus service systems on the environments in which individuals are functioning. This should serve to document the types of care that families are providing to their children, includ-ing adults with mental retardation. This description of the settings in which the person receives services will begin to build the typology of supports needed by the individual and the family.

THE IMPORTANCE OF CLINICAL JUDGMENT AND DECISION-MAKING

The decision-making necessary for establishing the diagnosis of mental retardation, which includes documentation of the levels of adaptive skills, also begins the process of reviewing existing supports and, as such, serves to begin the process presently referred to as "service planning" or "individual habilitation planning." The decision-making necessary to determine the intensities of needed supports requires clinical judgment, must include observation, and must emphasize natural environments and age-appropriate settings and opportunities.

AGE OF ONSET

Defining mental retardation as occurring before age 18 will serve to create uniformity across mental retardation delivery systems that have interpreted the previous age of onset criterion with a fair degree of variability. States have differentially operationalized the previously used term of *developmental period* to mean onset at different ages. The age-specific cutoff for the onset of mental retardation will serve to distinguish between mental retardation and other substantial limitations that may have somewhat similar behavioral manifestations but that occur after age 18. These other conditions, typically occurring during the late adolescent to young adult period, are usually ascribable to traumatic brain injury, for example, brain injury resulting from vehicular accidents.

LEGISLATIVE CHANGES

The definition will provide an opportunity for states to assure uniformity in legislation and regulation governing eligibility and the provision of supports to individuals with mental retardation and their families. State Medicaid plans and regulations, including the application and plan for the ICF/MR Community Care Waiver, may also need to be adapted to conform with the new definition.

CHALLENGES OF THE DEFINITION

RECONCEPTUALIZING DECISION-MAKING

The Definition, Classification, and Systems of Supports presents three specific sets of decisions to be made by service systems for individuals with, or suspected of having, mental retardation. The decisions to be made are: (a) diagnosis of mental retardation; (b) classification and description; and (c) determination of systems of supports. The construction of these decision points as separate determinations serves to make the process more functional for each person, based on individual abilities and needs, as well as contribute to the process of describing the environments and supports necessary. The three discrete decisions are made in the context of Intellectual Functioning and Adaptive Skills, Psychological/Emotional Considerations; Physical/Health/Etiology Considerations; and Environmental Considerations. The diagnosis of mental retardation is either made in the eligibility determination or verified as part of the determination process. The third decision, regarding the needed systems of supports, may be made by an agency or delivery system either during the eligibility process or as part of the planning for the provision of supports and services.

To apply the decision-making, we might consider some examples of adults with mental retardation and their needs for supports:

Mr. S. Mr. S is a 50-year-old man with Down syndrome whose only close relative, his 84-year-old mother, is dying of congestive heart failure. Although he completed elementary school in a "trainable" class placement, he has spent most of his adult life at home with his mother. He is known around the community but has depended on his mother's guidance for structuring his day. He has helped with household tasks but needs prompts to initiate and finish them.

During his mother's hospitalizations, an elderly neighbor has taken Mr. S into her home, but she is getting too frail to do that for any prolonged period of time. A hospital social worker, meeting Mr. S when he was brought to visit his mother by the neighbor, referred him to the state Office of Mental Retardation services. An intake evaluation was performed, including a psychological evaluation, physical exam, and home visit with Mr. S, his mother, and the neighbor.

The following decisions were made: Mr. S has mental retardation. (This decision was based on his IQ of 52, the childhood onset (trainable class placement), and his significant limitations in adaptive skills (social skills, self-direction, community use, and functional academics).

Mr. S has extensive needs for supports. Table 11.1 presents the specific supports needed by Mr. S and his mother at this time. Mr. S is not working, and he could be. Note that because of his mother's age and health and the age and health of his natural supports system (his neighbor), the supports needed by Mr. S and his family are paid supports (i.e., services, both generic and specialized).

Ms. V. Ms. V is a 24-year-old woman with mental retardation who has been a client of the Division of Mental Retardation since she was 12 years old. She has significant limitations in all adaptive skill areas. In addition to mental retardation, she has severe athetoid cerebral palsy, is blind, and has chronic pulmonary problems.

TABLE 11.1 Supports Needed by Mr. S

Dimension/Support focus area	Specific supports
I. Intellectual Functioning and Adaptive Skills	
Social skills	Assistance from homemaker
Self-direction	Life skills training from voluntary agency
	Evaluation for money management; assistance in decision-making
Community use	To be incorporated in supported living arrangement being planned
Work	Develop supported employment position
II: Psychological/ Emotional Considerations	Preparation to understand mother's illness and impending death
	Transition to a new home
Friendship	Maintain continuity with neighbor and her son
III: Physical/Health/Etiology Considerations	Primary health care; health maintenance and screenings
IV. Environmental Considerations	Provide round-the-clock homemaker/ nurse to maintain mother and son at home
	Planning for supervised living arrangement

Ms. V lives with her parents and an older adult sister and brother. Her other brother and his wife live down the block with their two teen-age children. When her parents need a break, she stays with her brother and sister-in-law. Although she used to attend an adult day program, her pulmonary problems forced her to miss so many days she is no longer enrolled.

At her annual Individual Habilitation Planning meeting, Ms. V's family, her case manager, and a representative from the Visiting Nurse Association agreed that her needs for supports continue to be extensive. She is not involved in any work program. Her needed supports are described in Table 11.2. Although her supports needs are extensive, Ms. S receives most of her supports through her natural and family networks, relying secondarily on generic and some specialized services.

TABLE 11.2 Supports Needed by Ms. V

Dimension/Support focus area	Specific supports
I. Intellectual Functioning and Adaptive Skills	Complete personal care assistance Adapted wheelchair Explore activities for community presence, opportunities for exercising choice and for work
II. Psychological/Emotional Considerations	None
III. Physical/Health/Etiology Considerations	Health maintenance Consultation with pulmonologist Respiratory therapy-train family Bi-weekly visiting nurse visits Positioning for contractures to enhance respiratory capacity
IV. Environmental Considerations	Adaptation of parents' house and brother's house to provide increased accessibility Facilitate visit of friends from former day program Evaluate for augmentative communication device Explore future living arrangement that would promote interdependence, but would be more independent of her family

THE ENVIRONMENT: IMPLICATIONS FOR PLACEMENT AND PROGRAMMING

Community environments form the context for the existence of limitations in adaptive skills, one of the three criteria for mental retardation. The assessment of adaptive skills must take place in reference to community environments that are typical for the person's chronological age. Once the diagnosis of mental retardation is established, environmental considerations are reviewed. Present settings and the optimal environment for the individual are to be reviewed and assessed on the basis of the extent to which these settings facilitate community integration. The concept of community is inextricably embedded in the definition of mental retardation.

Community emerges in this classification as the only meaningful context in which to discuss mental retardation. Mental retardation, as a diagnosis, has evolved from a description of individual functioning independent of setting to a description of individual functioning that can only be made within the context of community life. Previously institutionalized individuals, moving to the community and now receiving supports in the community, will continue to require the clinical decision-making necessary to establish the disability and intensities of needed supports.

MAXIMIZING SUPPORTS

Intensities of needed supports. Severity of disability has been excluded from the definition. Level of intellectual functioning does not determine a degree of limitations or access to particular types of services, particularly community settings. In some states, individuals who functioned within the more impaired ranges of mental retardation have been considered less appropriate for community placement and have had no service options other than institutional placement if their families could no longer provide sufficient supports to maintain them at home. The definition removes the assumptive base for service grouping by level and facilitates a reconceptualization of service delivery.

The methodology of removing the degree of limitations from the intensities of supports needed by the individual and the family should serve to minimize the tendencies, particularly of large delivery systems, to develop services or programs that are targeted or even restricted to individuals at a particular level of functioning.

Adoption of the definition by educational systems should contribute to minimizing some of the roadblocks between services for children and adult services and should enhance the transition from school to work. Utilizing a support paradigm also has the potential for minimizing or eliminating discontinuities for families, as natural supports do not follow the same rhythms or patterns as paid supports, which may be under the auspices of separate bureaucracies. The following example of Mr. T, a young adult with mental retardation beginning to make the transition from school to work, illustrates some of these continuities.

Mr. T. Mr. T is 20 years old, has mental retardation, and is presently job sampling through his educational placement to identify the type of job he would like to work at on a permanent basis. He lives with his family in a semi-rural area, attends the same high school as his younger sister, and, like his sister, travels there by school bus. He spends half his day in special education, the other part in typical classes oriented toward work study opportunities. His supports needs, which are limited, are now largely met by his family and neighbors; they are natural supports. As he makes the transition to work, his supports needs will remain limited, but they will shift, at least initially, to more paid supports for job coach services and specialized transportation services to work because there is no public transportation in his county. Eventually, Mr. T would like to move to a supported living arrangement and be more independent of his family. The teacher paraprofessional from his special education program and her husband are part of Mr. T's circle of support, which meets to help him plan his future. This couple, although not part of the formal adult service system, is discussing with Mr. T and his family how they might jointly create a shared living arrangement in which they could provide support to Mr. T Table 11.3 displays Mr. T's needs and supports.

TABLE 11.3   Supports Needed by Mr. T

Dimension/Support focus area	Specific supports
I: Intellectual Functioning and Adaptive Skills	
Functional academics	Continue school placement
Work	Continue job sampling
II: Psychological/ Emotional Considerations	None
III: Physical/Health/Etiology Considerations	Health maintenance as per age
IV: Environmental Considerations	Continue circle of support for personal futures planning; as Mr. T moves into a job, consider adding friends or colleagues from job

The Support Paradigm

Individual supports are crucial to the conceptualization of mental retardation. They can be put in place by the family, significant others and service providers, or agencies to address limitations in adaptive skills. It is the provision of these supports in appropriate combination and of sufficient duration that may enhance the adaptive functioning of the individual. Supports can be conceptualized in concentric circles, with the individual and the family in the center of the circle (see Figure 11.1).

FIGURE 11.1   The Nature of Systems of Supports

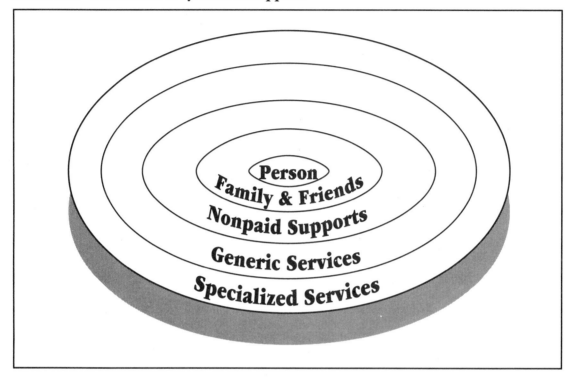

Supports can be what the family or other people who are not paid provide to the individual or they may be provided to the family to enhance their capacity to compensate for limitations in particular skill areas. The provision of paid services, by public or private agencies, can be viewed as a subset of supports or as a type of support. Previously, delivery systems for adults have viewed the services they provide as the only significant component of habilitation.

The supports paradigm represents a shift from reliance on program models, where individuals are forced to "fit into" existing services to service delivery that is more individually based and tailored. Examples of these shifts are supported employment (Bellamy, Rhodes, Mank, and Albin, 1988; Kiernan and Stark, 1986) and supported living (Bradley and Knoll, 1990; G. Smith, 1990). Supports coordination, while typically a paid service, can be an important cornerstone in accessing needed supports, especially paid services (Sullivan and Spitalnik, 1988). The definition in this manual places increased demands on the services coordinator to focus on both capabilities and limitations and to coordinate individually driven support and service constellations. Although most service systems have planning processes to develop individual plans, either IHPs (Individual Habilitation Plans) or ISPs (Individual Service Plans), most of these plans are oriented to fitting individuals into existing service models and options. Most of these planning processes are system driven rather than individually or consumer driven.

More consonant with the support approach inherent in the Definition, Classification, and Systems of Supports presented in this manual is a variety of strategies that have been developed for implementing more person-centered approaches to planning, including personal futures planning (O'Brien and Lyle, 1987), functional life planning or 24-hour planning (Green-McGowan and Kovacs, 1984), and the kaleidoscope (Forest and Lusthaus, 1988).

THE IMPROVEMENT OF FUNCTION

Mental retardation typically persists throughout the life span. The definition in this manual recognizes that "with appropriate supports over a sustained period, the life functioning of the person with mental retardation will generally improve."

The improvement in life functioning represents an improvement in adaptive skills. This improvement may be dependent upon the continued provision of existing supports or represent developmental progress that may make possible the gradual fading of more intensive supports in favor of less intensive supports. Improvement in life functioning may also shift the balance between paid supports and more natural supports. An example of supported employment illustrates this evolution: from intensive job coaching, to the job coach fading in the intensity and duration of support visits, to another employee becoming the support with perhaps periodic visits from the job coach to check in.

One of the critical elements in assuring that supports remain in place and evolve in a developmentally appropriate manner is on-going access to the type of clinical decision-making that forms the basis of the multidimensional classification process (chapter 3). In addition, developers of service systems need to make a commitment to the provision of needed supports to individuals rather than depending on individual needs being addressed through the movement of a person along a fixed continuum of service models.

For individuals whose needs for supports lessen as their adaptive skills increase, delivery systems need to offer flexibility in the type, extent, and duration of supports offered. Permitting individuals to maintain access to particular or discrete components of supports may be the critical element in enhancing or maintaining adaptive functioning. Conversely, the loss of those supports may produce a decrement in adaptive skills such that more extensive supports would then again be required. To assure these balances, the system or provider must continue to maintain a focus on the individual, not on groups or "types" of clients; provide continued access, as needed, to clinical decision-making; and have mechanisms such as service coordination. If the individual and family wishes, service providers can maintain on-going periodic contact to both track the adequacy and appropriateness of supports and serve as a link to other supports when necessary. Individual preferences and wishes for the type of support or for any connection to the systems of paid supports must be respected. There must always be on-going access for people to return to supports as their individual needs, family circumstances, or environments change. The decision for individuals to leave the paid service system should only be seen as final as these individuals wish it to be.

GREATER SPECIFICITY

The movement to eliminate categories for describing the degree of limitation and provide four categories for describing the intensities of needed supports is not intended to introduce less specificity into decision-making. Rather, with the increased reliance on clinical judgment and decision-making and individualized addressing of needs, the intent is to introduce more specificity, but in a consumer-driven way, which by definition must be individualized.

RECONCEPTUALIZING SERVICE DELIVERY

Delivery systems must reorient their roles from being providers of program services to being providers and facilitators of individual supports. The definition requires an increase in clinical decision-making and individual specificity in contrast to categorical or arbitrary skill groupings. Delivery systems must continue to shift away from reliance on program models and service continua to developing supports systems. Service provision by delivery systems should focus on the structured facilitation of access to generic services and, where necessary, on the development of specialized services. Specialized services must be organized as individual and family supports: integrated employment options, supported living options, respite and other family supports, and other nonfacility based services that enhance the community integration of people with mental retardation. Service provision should supplement natural supports and enhance the development of adaptive skills. The reorientation in service delivery to adults occasioned by the definition in this manual will enhance the opportunities for the expression of the capacities and capabilities of people with mental retardation.

CHAPTER 12

SOCIAL POLICY AND LEGAL APPLICATIONS

Any change in the formulation of terminology and classification in mental retardation affects important issues in the lives of individuals with mental retardation and their families; the field of mental retardation; and related service delivery, social policy governmental, and legal areas. During the transition to the 1992 AAMR Definition, Classification, and Systems of Supports, professionals and others will need to learn about the conceptualization reflected in the manual in which mental retardation is viewed as an interaction of the person and the environment, in which the person's functioning is the critical measure, in which the concept of adaptive behavior has been extended to 10 adaptive skill areas, and in which classification is focused on the needed systems of supports. Because of the important implications of the new conceptualization in this chapter, we discuss three critical policy and legal issues involved in implementing the new system: eligibility and funding for services, research, and legal practices.

ELIGIBILITY AND FUNDING FOR SERVICES

One of the evolving practices in the field of mental retardation is the increasing use of daily life functioning as the measure of limitations and need for supports. This practice is particularly evident in the evolution of the definition of developmental disabilities in children used by the Social Security Administration. Originally conceptualized as a simple level of impairment attributed to a particular medical condition, the definition of *disability* in a child under age 18 is now conceptualized in terms of functional limitations in many life activities.

For most individuals mental retardation is of lifelong duration, and their needs for systems of supports will continue through their lives. For some individuals, however, mental retardation may not be of lifelong duration—a diagnosis of mental retardation made at an earlier time may not be applicable at a later time. This situation might arise in several ways. These include:

- *Mistaken diagnosis:* An earlier diagnosis may have been simply inaccurate, as in the case of an infant or very young child for whom accurate diagnosis is especially difficult or the case where the earlier diagnosis was applied by a professional insufficiently skilled or experienced in mental retardation.
- *Intervention*: An earlier diagnosis may have been accurate at the time it was applied, but specialized habilitation services or medical care or treatment (such as for severe seizure disorders) cured the individual.

- *Improved adaptive skills and assimilation*: The individual has, over time, assimilated into his or her natural environment, no longer requires supports, and can maintain adequate functioning without supports in new environments as they arise.

This latter case is likely only when the individual's assessed functioning was marginally outside "normal" intelligence, at the upper limits of mental retardation, and/or when the present environment is cognitively undemanding or particularly tolerant. This should not be confused with a case where the individual is being provided supports that allow him or her to function presently without substantial limitations, but for whom mental retardation remains an underlying limitation that will surface with the withdrawal of supports. Neither should it be confused with a case where the individual is assimilated into his or her environment, but new environments or challenges cause the underlying mental retardation to surface.

This cure or elimination of the presenting problems associated with mental retardation in an individual should be a positive event. Tragically, several major risks accompany possible improvement in functioning. Thus, policy makers and practitioners need to be vigilant against risks such as the premature removal of supports through inappropriate practices, for example (a) mistakenly removing as "no longer needed" the very systems of supports that are allowing the improvement; (b) requiring that individuals with mental retardation repeatedly "re-prove" the disability, thereby discouraging applicants and cutting back on the number of recipients of services; and (c) inaccurately interpreting as a cure improvements in functioning in an undemanding or tolerant environment that do not generalize to more demanding environments. Consider the following examples as elaborations of these risks.

Albert. Albert was born prematurely. He was diagnosed immediately after birth as being significant developmentally delayed and having mental retardation. He was later than 97 percent of the population in achieving all the major developmental milestones. Albert received early intervention services in a special preschool, attended a developmental kindergarten, and received special education in first grade. Gradually, Albert caught up with his age peers. By second grade, he was successfully completing school work on his grade level. His mental retardation was not of lifelong duration.

Becca. Becca was born with spina bifida and hydrocephaly. She was diagnosed as having mental retardation at the time of birth by the delivery nurse. Becca received antibiotics and immediate surgery to close the lesion, preventing central nervous system infection. She also received a shunt that drained the excess cerebrospinal fluid from her brain to her abdominal area. Becca received necessary orthopedic surgeries and physical therapy over the next several years. She entered the public school system, was evaluated, and found to have a "normal" IQ. Becca's initial diagnosis of mental retardation was made prematurely and was incorrect.

Caren. Caren was accurately classified as having mental retardation throughout her elementary and secondary schooling. After graduating with a certificate of completion, she moved to an isolated farm in a rural part of the state with her new husband. She was not known to the mental retardation service providers in the area. She generally kept to herself, except for church attendance. She helped with all the farm work, and when her husband was away from the farm, she conducted most of the chores. One day her husband was found dead in their bed. Caren was arrested for homicide. She was substantially limited in her ability to function with the police or in the criminal justice system. Caren's mental retardation was of lifelong duration.

David. Since he was 3 years old, David has been classified as having mental retardation. He is now 30, lives with a roommate in an apartment near his work, and attends all the home games of the city's professional baseball team. His mother cleans his apartment two times per month and pays all his bills. David works as a janitor at a neighborhood fast food restaurant. His father takes him to and from work. A social worker visits him once per month and occasionally talks with David's employer to make sure that he continues to perform his job well. With these supports David is able to function presently without substantial limitations. David's mental retardation is of lifelong duration.

RESEARCH

We anticipate that the 1992 Definition, Classification, and Systems of Supports will challenge the research community. For example, a major anticipated change is the description of research subjects. The new system requires greater precision in the description of subjects beyond the mild, moderate, severe, and profound categorization. Now practice will demand complete information on the person's assessed level of intellectual functioning (IQ), a profile of adaptive skills, the condition's etiology, and the types and intensities of supports needed by—and provided to—the person.

A second anticipated change relates to focusing on the assets and liabilities of the person's environment and the types and intensities of supports being received by the person. As a result, there will be less emphasis on the person's condition and functioning level as the independent variable. Rather, more emphasis will be given to environmental conditions and support structures as independent or intervening variables and the person's functioning level, living/employment status, or level of satisfaction as the dependent variable.

In addition to the ongoing research in typical areas, and lines of research currently underway, some researchers should turn their attention to large utilization studies and large-scale field testing of the definition so that its effects, if any, can be monitored.

LEGAL PRACTICES

Some legal cases can be affected when a participant has a diagnosis of mental retardation. A diagnosis can alert lawyers, judges, and other justice personnel that a participant (for example, a petitioner or respondent, or defendant) is eligible for certain services or accommodations or is entitled to certain legal protections based on the diagnosis.

In the past, particularly in criminal cases, diagnoses have sometimes been challenged because the concept of adaptive behavior could not be precisely defined. Its extension in this definition to 10 adaptive skill areas should lessen the problem.

TRANSITION TO CHANGE FOR THE DEFINITION

Past experience teaches that governmental entities cannot change definitions overnight. The time required to complete a change varies according to many variables, but Lowitzer, Utley, and Baumeister (1987) reported delay in adopting the 1983 definition. A change of this type requires time. Even as here, where the change extends and builds on the previous definition and attempts to respond to and incorporate many changes already in practice, some time delay should be anticipated.

REFERENCES

A

Aase, J. M. (1990). *Diagnostic dysmorphology.* New York: Plenum.

Adams, G. L. (1984). *Comprehensive Test of Adaptive Behavior.* Columbus, OH: Merrill.

American Psychiatric Association. (1987). *Diagnostic and statistical manual of mental disorders* (3rd ed., revised [DSM-III-R]). Washington, DC: Author.

American Psychiatric Association. (in press). *Diagnostic and statistical manual of mental disorders* (4th ed. [DSM-IV]). Washington, DC: Author.

Argan, M., & Martin, J. (1985). Establishing socially validated drug research in community settings. *Psychopharmacology Bulletin, 21,* 285–290.

B

Baumeister, A. A. (1987). Mental retardation: Some conceptions and dilemmas. *American Psychologist, 42,* 796–800.

Baumgart, D., & Ferguson, D. L. (1991). Personnel preparation: Directions for the next decade. In L. H. Meyer, C. A. Peck, & L. Brown (Eds.), *Critical issues in the lives of people with severe disabilities* (pp. 313–352). Baltimore: Brookes.

Bellamy, G. T. (1990). Book review. *Journal of the Association for Persons with Severe Handicaps, 15,* 261–265.

Bellamy, G. T., Newton, J. S., LeBaron, N., & Horner, R. H. (1990). Quality of life and lifestyle outcomes: A challenge for residential programs. In R. L. Schalock (Ed.), *Quality of life: Perspectives and issues* (pp. 127–137). Washington, DC: American Association on Mental Retardation.

Bellamy, G. T., Rhodes, L. E., Mank, D. M., & Albin, J. M. (1988). *Supported employment: A community implementation guide.* Baltimore: Brookes.

Blatt, B. (1987). *The conquest of mental retardation.* Austin, TX: Pro-Ed.

Blunden, R. (1988). Program features of quality services. In M. P. Janicki, M. M. Krauss, & M. Seltzer (Eds.), *Community residences for persons with developmental disabilities: Here to stay* (pp. 117–122). Baltimore: Brookes.

Borthwick, S. A. (1988). Maladaptive behavior among the mentally retarded: The need for reliable data. In J. A. Stark, F. J. Menolascino, M. H. Albarelli, & V. C. Gray (Eds.), *Mental retardation and mental health: Classification, diagnosis, treatment, services.* (pp. 30–40). New York: Springer-Verlag.

Borthwick-Duffy, S., & Eyman, R. K. (1990). Who are the dually diagnosed? *American Journal on Mental Retardation, 94,* 586–595.

Braddock, D., Hemp, R., Fujiura, G. Backelder, L., & Mitchell, D. (1990). *The state of the states in developmental disabilities.* Baltimore: Brookes.

Bradley, V., & Knoll, J. (1990). *Shifting paradigms in services to people with developmental disabilities.* Cambridge, MA: Human Services Research Institute.

Bronfenbrenner, U. (1979). *The ecology of human development.* Cambridge: Harvard University Press.

Browder, D. M. (1991). *Assessment of individuals with severe disabilities* (2nd ed.). Baltimore: Brookes.

Browder, D. M., & Snell, M. E. (1988). Assessment of individuals with severe handicaps. In E. S. Shapiro & T. R. Kratchowill (Eds.), *Behavioral assessment in schools: Conceptual foundations and practice applications* (pp. 121–160). New York: Guilford Press.

Bruininks, R., & McGrew, K. (1987). *Exploring the structure of adaptive behavior.* Minneapolis: University of Minnesota Press.

Bruininks, R. H., Thurlow, M., & Gilman, C. J. (1987). Adaptive behavior and mental retardation. *Journal of Special Education, 21,* 69–88.

Bruininks, R. H., Woodcock, R. W., Weatherman, R. F., & Hill, B. K. (1984). *Scales of Independent Behavior.* Allen, TX: DLM/Teaching Resources.

Buyse, M. L. (Ed.). (1990). *Birth defects encyclopedia.* Dover, MA: Center for Birth Defects Information Services.

C

Conoley, J. C., & Kramer, J. J. (1989). *Tenth mental measurements yearbook.* Lincoln, NE: Buros.

Conroy, J. W. (1985). Medical needs of institutionalized mentally retarded persons: Perceptions of families and staff members. *American Journal of Mental Deficiency, 89,* 510–514.

Conroy, J., & Bradley, V. J. (1985). *The Pennhurst longitudinal study: A report of five years of research and analysis.* Philadelphia: Temple University, Developmental Disabilities Center.

Conroy, J., Efthimiou, J., & Lemanowicz, J. (1982). A matched comparison of the developmental growth of de-institutionalized mentally retarded clients. *American Journal of Mental Deficiency, 86,* 581–587.

Coulter, D. L. (1987). The neurology of mental retardation. In F. J. Menolascino & J. A. Stark (Eds.), *Preventive and curative intervention in mental retardation* (pp. 113–152). Baltimore: Brookes.

Coulter, D. L. (1990). Home is the place: Quality of life for young children with developmental disabilities. In R. L. Schalock (Ed.), *Quality of life: Perspectives and issues* (pp. 61-70). Washington, DC: American Association on Mental Retardation.

Coulter, D. L. (1991a). Approaches to ethics. In J. A. Mulick & R. A. Antonak (Eds.), *Transitions in mental retardation* (Vol. 5, pp. 115-121). New York: Ablex.

Coulter, D. L. (1991b). The failure of prevention. *Mental Retardation, 29,* 3-4.

Danielson, L. C., & Bellamy, G. T. (1989). State variation in placement of children with handicaps in segregated environments. *Exceptional Children, 55,* 448-455.

D

Davis, D. R. (1988). Nutrition in the prevention and reversal of mental retardation. In F. J. Menolascino & J. A. Stark (Eds.), *Prevention and curative intervention in mental retardation* (pp. 177-219). Baltimore: Brookes.

DeJong, R. N. (1979). *The neurological examination* (4th ed.). Hagerstown, MD: Harper & Row.

DeLaurin, K. (1990). Judgment-based assessment: Making the implicit explicit. *Topics in Early Childhood Special Education, 10*(3), 96-110.

Dodrill, C. B., & Troupin, A. S. (1991). Neuropsychological effects of carbamazepine and phenytoin: A reanalysis. *Neurology, 41,* 141-143.

Doll, E. A. (1953). *Vineland Social Maturity Scale.* Minneapolis: American Guidance Service.

Duncan, D., Sbardellati, E., Maheady, L., & Sainato, D. (1981). Nondiscriminatory assessment of severely physically handicapped individuals. *Journal of the Association for the Severely Handicapped, 6,* 17-22.

Durand, V. M., & Crimmins, D. B. (1988). Identifying the variables maintaining self-injurious behavior. *Journal of Autism and Developmental Disorders, 18,* 99-117.

Durand, V. M., & Kishi, G. (1987). Reducing severe behavior problems among persons with dual sensory impairments: An evaluation of a technical assistance model. *Journal of the Association for Persons with Severe Handicaps, 12,* 2-10.

E

Edgerton, R. B. (1988). Community adaptation of people with mental retardation. In J. F. Kavanagh (Ed.), *Understanding mental retardation: Research accomplishment and new frontiers* (pp. 311-318). Baltimore: Brookes.

Elstein, A., Shulman, L., & Sprafka, S. (1978). *Medical problem solving.* Cambridge: Harvard University Press.

Erikson, E. H. (1950). *Childhood and society.* New York: Norton.

Evans, I. M. (1990). Testing and diagnosis: A review and evaluation. In L. H. Meyer, C. A. Peck, & L. Brown (Eds.), *Critical issues in the lives of people with severe disabilities* (pp. 25-44). Baltimore: Brookes.

Eyman, R. K., Grossman, H. J., Chaney, R. H., & Call, T. L. (1990). The life expectancy of profoundly handicapped people with mental retardation. *New England Journal of Medicine, 323,* 584-589.

F

Farwell, J. R., Lee, Y. J., Hirtz, D. G., Sulzbacher, S. I., Ellenberg, J. H., & Nelson, K. B. (1990). Phenobarbital for febrile seizures: Effects on intelligence and on seizure recurrence. *New England Journal of Medicine, 322,* 364-369.

Feingold, M., & Pashayan, H. (1983). *Genetics and birth defects in clinical practice.* Boston: Little, Brown.

Fine, M. A., Tangeman, P. J., & Woodward, J. (1990). Changes in adaptive behavior of older adults with mental retardation following deinstitutionalization. *American Journal on Mental Retardation, 94,* 661-668.

Fiorelli, J. S., & Thurman, S. K. (1979). Client behavior in more or less normalized residential settings. *Education and Training of the Mentally Retarded, 14*(2), 85-94.

Flanagan, J. C. (1978). A research approach to improving our quality of life. *American Psychologist, 33,* 138-147.

Fletcher, R. J. (1988). A county systems model: Comprehensive services for the dually diagnosed. In J. A. Stark, F. J. Menolascino, M. H. Albarelli, & V. C. Gray (Eds.), *Mental retardation and mental health: Classification, diagnosis, treatment, services* (pp. 122-137). New York: Springer-Verlag.

Ford, A., Davern, L., & Schnorr, R. (1992). Inclusive education: "Making sense" of the curriculum. In S. Stainback & W. Stainback (Eds.), *Curriculum considerations in inclusive classrooms* (pp. 37-61). Baltimore: Brookes.

Ford, A., Schnorr, R., Meyer, L., Davern, L., Black, J., & Dempsey, P. (1989). *The Syracuse community-referenced curriculum guide.* Baltimore: Brookes.

Ford, A., Schnorr, R., Meyer, L., Davern, L., Black, J., & Dempsey, P. (1990). Judgment-based assessment: Making the implicit explicit. *Topics in Early Childhood Special Education, 10*(3), 96-110.

Forest, M. (1991). It's about relationships. In L. H. Meyer, C. A. Peck, & L. Brown (Eds.), *Critical issues in the lives of people with severe disabilities* (pp. 399-408). Baltimore: Brookes.

Forest, M., & Lusthaus, E. (1988). *The kaleidoscope: Each belongs—quality education for all.* Unpublished manuscript, Frontier College, Toronto.

Forest, M., & Snow, J. *The MAPS process.* Ontario: Frontier College.

Frankenberger, W., & Harper, J. (1988). States' definitions and procedures for identifying children with mental retardation: Comparison of 1981-1982 and 1985-1986 guidelines. *Mental Retardation, 26,* 133-136.

Fuchs, D., & Fuchs, L. (1989). Exploring effective and efficient pre-referral interventions: A component analysis of behavioral consultation. *School Psychological Review, 18,* 260-279.

Furlong, M. J., & LeDrew, L. (1985). IQ = 68 = mildly retarded? Factors influencing multidisciplinary team recommendations on children with FS IQs between 63 and 75. *Psychology in the Schools, 22,* 5-9.

G

Galler, J. R. (1988). The intergenerational effects of undernutrition. In J. F. Kavanagh (Ed.), *Understanding mental retardation: Research accomplishments and new frontiers* (pp. 35-40). Baltimore: Brookes.

Garber, H. L. (1988). *The Milwaukee Project: Preventing mental retardation in children at risk.* Washington, DC: American Association on Mental Retardation.

Gardner, H. (1983). *Frames of mind: The theory of multiple intelligences.* New York: Basic Books.

Garrard, S. D. (1982). Health services for mentally retarded people in community residences: Problems and questions. *American Journal of Public Health, 72,* 1226-1228.

Gartner, A., & Lipsky, D. K. (1987). Beyond special education: Toward a quality system for all students. *Harvard Educational Review, 57,* 367-395.

Giangreco, M. F., & Putnam, J. W. (1991). Supporting the education of students with severe disabilities in regular education environments. In L. H. Meyer, C. A. Peck, & L. Brown (Eds.), *Critical issues in the lives of people with severe disabilities* (pp. 245-270). Baltimore: Brookes.

Giangreco, M. F., York, J., & Rainforth, B. (1989). Providing related services to learners with severe handicaps in educational settings: Pursuing the least restrictive option. *Pediatric Physical Therapy, 1(2),* 55-63.

Googins, B. (1989). Support in integrated work settings: The role played by industry through employee assistance programs. In W. E. Kiernan & R. L. Schalock (Eds.), *Economics, industry, and disability: A look ahead* (pp. 223-236). Baltimore: Brookes.

Graden, J. L., & Bauer, A. M. (1992). Using a collaborative approach to support students and teachers in inclusive classrooms. In S. Stainback & W. Stainback (Eds.), *Curriculum considerations in inclusive classrooms* (pp. 85-100). Baltimore: Brookes.

Greenspan, S. (1979). Social intelligence in the retarded. In N. R. Ellis (Ed.), *Handbook of mental deficiency: Psychological theory and research* (2nd ed., pp. 1–89). Hillsdale, NJ: Erlbaum.

Greenspan, S. (1981). Defining childhood social competence: A proposed working model. In B. K. Keogh (Ed.), *Advances in special education* (Vol. 3, pp. 1–39). Greenwich, CT: JAI Press.

Greenspan, S. (1990). *A redefinition of mental retardation based on a revised model of social competence.* Paper presented at the annual meeting of the American Association on Mental Retardation, Atlanta.

Gresham, F. M., & Elliott, S. N. (1987). The relationship between adaptive behavior and social skills: Issues in definition and assessment. *Journal of Special Education, 21,* 167–181.

Grossman, H. J. (Ed.). (1983). *Classification in mental retardation.* Washington, DC: American Association on Mental Deficiency.

Gualtieri, C. T. (1988). Mental health of persons with mental retardation: A solution, obstacles to the solution, and a resolution for the problem. In J. A. Stark, F. J. Menolascino, M. H. Albarelli, & V. C. Gray (Eds.), *Mental retardation and mental health: Classification, diagnosis, treatment, services* (pp. 112–121). New York: Springer-Verlag.

Guilford, J. P. (1967). *The nature of human intelligence.* New York: McGraw-Hill.

H

Haring, T. G., & Breen, C. (1989). Units of analysis of social interaction outcomes in supported education. *Journal of the Association for Persons with Severe Handicaps, 14,* 255–262.

Harrison, P. L. (1987). Research with adaptive behavior scales. *Journal of Special Education, 21,* 37–68.

Hawkins, G. D., & Cooper, D. H. (1990). Adaptive behavior measures in mental retardation research: Subject description in AJMD/AJMR articles (1979–1987). *American Journal on Mental Retardation, 94,* 654–660.

Heber, R. (1959). A manual on terminology and classification in mental retardation. *American Journal of Mental Deficiency, 64* (Monograph Supplement).

Helmstetter, E. (1989). Curriculum for school-age students: An ecological model. In F. Brown & D. H. Lehr (Eds.), *Persons with profound disabilities: Issues and practices* (pp. 239–263). Baltimore: Brookes.

Hill, B., Balow, E., & Bruininks, R. (1985). A national study of prescribed drugs in institutions and community residential facilities for mentally retarded people. *Psychopharmacology Bulletin, 21,* 279–284.

Horner, R. H., Dunlap, G., Koegel, R. L., Carr, E. G., Sailor, W., Anderson, J., Albin, R. W., & O'Neill, R. E. (1990). Toward a technology of "nonaversive" behavioral support. *Journal of the Association for Persons with Severe Handicaps, 15*, 60–69.

Howard, A. (1991, March). *Financing health care for youth and adults with developmental disabilities.* Paper presented at a conference on Health Care for Youth and Adults With Developmental Disabilities: Policies and Partnerships, Bethesda, MD.

Huefner, D. S. (1988). The consulting teacher model: Risks and opportunities. *Exceptional Children, 54,* 403–414.

Hughes, C., Rusch, F. R., & Curl, R. M. (1990). Extending individual competence, development of natural support, and promoting social acceptance. In F. R. Rusch (Ed.), *Supported employment: Models, methods, and issues* (pp. 181–197). Sycamore, IL: Sycamore.

Huttenlocher, P. R. (1991). Dendritic and synaptic pathology in mental retardation. *Pediatric Neurology, 7,* 79–85.

I

Institute of Medicine. (1991). *Disability in America: Toward a national agenda for prevention.* Washington, DC: National Academy Press.

J

Jacobson, J. W. (1990). Do some mental disorders occur less frequently among persons with mental retardation. *American Journal on Mental Retardation, 94,* 596–602.

Jones, K. L. (1988). *Smith's recognizable patterns of human malformation* (4th ed.). Philadelphia: Saunders.

K

Kamphaus, R. W. (1987). Conceptual and psychometric issues in the assessment of adaptive behavior. *Journal of Special Education, 21,* 27–35.

Kanner, L. (1949). Miniature textbook of feeble-mindedness. *Child Care Monographs,* No. 1.

Kaufman, A. S., & Kaufman, N. L. (1983). *Kaufman Assessment Battery for Children.* Circle Pines, MN: American Guidance Service.

Kavanagh, J. F. (Ed.). (1988). *Understanding mental retardation: Research accomplishments and new frontiers.* Baltimore: Brookes.

Kennedy, C. H., Horner, R. H., Newton, J. S., & Kanda, E. (1990). Measuring the activity patterns of adults with severe disabilities using the resident lifestyle inventory. *Journal of the Association for Persons with Severe Handicaps, 15,* 79–85.

Keyes, D. (1990). *Issues in assessment theory and mental retardation.* Unpublished manuscript, University of New Mexico, Albuquerque.

Kidd, J. W. (1984). The 1983 AAMD definition and classification of mental retardation: The apparent impact of the CEC-MR position. *Education and Training of the Mentally Retarded, 18,* 243-244.

Kiernan, W. E., & McGaughey, M. (1991). *Employee assistance programs: A support mechanism for the worker with a disability.* Boston: Children's Hospital, Training and Research Institute for People with Disabilities.

Kiernan, W. E., Smith, B. C., & Ostrowsky, M. B. (1986). Developmental disabilities: Definitional issues. In W. E. Kiernan & J. A. Stark (Eds.), *Pathways to employment for adults with developmental disabilities* (pp. 11-20). Baltimore: Brookes.

Kiernan, W. E., & Stark, J. A. (Eds.). (1986). *Pathways to employment for adults with developmental disabilities.* Baltimore: Brookes.

Knoll, J. A. (1990). Defining quality in residential services. In V. J. Bradley & H. A. Bersani (Eds.), *Quality assurance for individuals with developmental disabilities: It's everybody's business* (pp. 235-261). Baltimore: Brookes.

Knoll, J., & Ford, A. (1987). Beyond caregiving: A reconceptualization of the role of the residential provider. In S. J. Taylor, D. Biklen, & J. Knoll (Eds.), *Community integration for people with severe disabilities.* New York: Teacher's College Press.

Koehler, R. S., Schalock, R. L., & Ballard, B. L. (1989). *Personal growth habilitation manual.* Hastings: Mid-Nebraska Mental Retardation Services.

L

Lambert, N. M., & Windmiller, M. B. (1981). *AAMD Adaptive Behavior Scale—School edition.* Monterey, CA: Publishers Test Service.

Landesman-Dwyer, S. (1981). Living in the community. *American Journal of Mental Deficiency, 86,* 223-234.

Landesman, S., & Ramey, C. (1989). Developmental psychology and mental retardation: Integrating scientific principles with treatment practices. *American Psychologist, 44,* 409-415.

Landesman, S., & Vietze, P. (Eds.). (1987). *Living environments and mental retardation.* Washington, DC: American Association on Mental Deficiency.

Laski, F. (1991). Achieving integration during the second revolution. In L. H. Meyer, C. A. Peck, & L. Brown (Eds.), *Critical issues in the lives of people with severe disabilities* (pp. 409-421). Baltimore: Brookes.

Lewis, M., & MacLean, W. (1982). Issues in treating emotional disorders. In J. Matson & R. Barrett (Eds.), *Psychopathology in the mentally retarded* (pp. 70-79). New York: Grune & Stratton.

Lipsky, D. K., & Gartner, A. (1991). Restructuring for quality. In J. W. Lloyd, N. N. Singh, & A. C. Repp (Eds.), *The Regular Education Initiative: Alternative perspectives on concepts, issues, and models* (pp. 43-56). Sycamore, IL: Sycamore.

Lloyd, J. W., Singh, N. N., & Repp, A. C. (1991). *The Regular Education Initiative: Alternative perspectives on concepts, issues, and models.* Sycamore, IL: Sycamore.

Lohman, D. F. (1989). Human intelligence: An introduction to advances in theory and research. *Review of Educational Research, 59,* 333-373.

Lowitzer, A. C., Utley, C. A., & Baumeister, A. A. (1987). AAMD's 1983 Classification in Mental Retardation as utilized by state mental retardation/developmental disabilities agencies. *Mental Retardation, 25,* 287-291.

M

MacMillan, D. L. (1989a). Equality, excellence and the EMR population: 1970-1989. *Psychology in Mental Retardation and Developmental Disabilities,* 15(2), 1-10.

MacMillan, D. L. (1989b). Mild mental retardation: Emerging issues. In G. Robinson, J. R. Patton, E. A. Polloway, & L. Sargent (Eds.), *Best practices in mild mental retardation* (pp.1-20). Reston, VA: CEC-M.

Martinez, C. (1990). A dream for myself. In R. Schalock (Ed.), *Quality of life: Perspectives and issues.* Washington, DC: American Association on Mental Retardation.

Masland, R. H. (1988). *Career research award address.* Paper presented at the annual meeting of the American Academy of Mental Retardation, Washington, DC.

McDonald, E. P. (1985). Medical needs of severely developmentally disabled persons residing in the community. *American Journal of Mental Deficiency, 90,* 171-176.

McDonnell, A. P., & Hardman, M. L. (1989). The desegregation of America's special schools: Strategies for change. *Journal of the Association for Persons with Severe Handicaps, 14,* 68-74.

McFadden, D. L., & Burke, E. P. (1991). Developmental disabilities and the new paradigm: Directions for the 1990s. *Mental Retardation, 29*(1), iii-vi.

McGrew, K., & Bruininks, R. (1989). The factor structure of adaptive behavior. *School Psychology Review, 18,* 64-81.

McGrew, K., & Bruininks, R. H. (1990). Defining adaptive and maladaptive behavior within a model of personal competence. *School Psychology Review, 19,* 53-73.

McLaren, J., & Bryson, S. E. (1987). Review of recent epidemiological studies of mental retardation: Prevalence, associated disorders, and etiology. *American Journal of Mental Retardation, 92,* 243-254.

Meacham, F. R., Kline, M. M., Stovall, J. A., & Sands, D. I. (1987). Adaptive behavior and low incidence handicaps: Hearing and visual impairments. *Journal of Special Education,* 21, 183-196.

Meador, D. M., Osborn, R. G., Owens, M. H., Smith, E. C., & Taylor, T. L. (1991). Evaluation of environmental support in group homes for persons with mental retardation. *Mental Retardation, 29,* 159-164.

Menolascino, F. (1977). *Challenges in mental retardation: Progressive ideology and services.* New York : Human Sciences Press.

Menolascino, F. (1988). Mental illness in the mentally retarded: Diagnostic and treatment issues. In J. A. Stark, F. J. Menolascino, M. A. Albarelli, & V. C. Gray (Eds.), *Mental retardation and mental health: Classification, diagnosis, treatment services* (pp. 150–162). New York: Springer-Verlag.

Menolascino, F. J., & Stark, J. A. (Eds.). (1984). *Handbook of mental illness in the mentally retarded.* New York: Plenum Press.

Menolascino, F. J., & Stark, J. A. (Eds.). (1988). *Preventive and curative intervention in mental retardation.* Baltimore: Brookes.

Mercer, J. R. (1973). The myth of 3% prevalence. In R. K. Eyman, C. E. Meyers, & G. Tarjan (Eds.), *Sociobehavioral studies in mental retardation.* Washington, DC: American Association on Mental Deficiency.

Mercer, J. R., & Lewis, J. P. (1977). *System of Multicultural Pluralistic Assessment: Parent interview manual.* New York: Psychological Corp.

Meyer, L. H., & Evans, I. M. (1989). *Nonaversive intervention for behavior problems.* Baltimore: Brookes.

Middleton, H. A., Keene, R. G., & Brown, G. W. (1990). Convergent discriminant validities of the Scales of Independent Behavior and the revised Vineland Adaptive Behavior Scales. *American Journal on Mental Retardation, 94,* 669–673.

Mount, B. (1987). *Personal futures planning: Finding directions for change.* New York: Graphic Futures.

N

Naisbitt, J., & Aburdene, P. (1990). *Megatrends 2000: Ten new directions for the 1990's* (pp. 290–321). New York: Avon Books.

Neel, R. S., & Billingsley, F. F. (1989). *Impact: A functional curriculum handbook for students with moderate to severe disabilities.* Baltimore: Brookes.

Neisworth, J., & Bagnato, S. J. (1988). Assessment in early childhood special education: A typology of dependent measures. In S. M. Odom & M. B. Karnes (Eds.), *Early intervention for infants and children with handicaps* (pp. 23–49). Baltimore: Brookes.

Nelson, J. R. (1984). *Human life: A biblical perspective for bioethics.* Philadelphia: Fortress Press.

Nevin, A., & Thousand, J. (1987). Avoiding or limiting special education referrals: Changes and challenges. In M. C. Wang, M. C. Reynolds, & H. J. Walberg (Eds.), *Handbook of special education: Research and practice* (pp. 273–286). New York: Pergamon Press.

Nihira, K., Foster, R., Shellhaas, M., & Leland, H. (1974). *Adaptive Behavior Scales.* Washington, DC: American Association on Mental Deficiency.

Nisbet, J., & Hagner, D. (1988). Natural supports in the workplace: A reexamination of supported employment. *Journal of the Association for Persons with Severe Handicaps, 13*, 260-267.

O

O'Brien, J. O. (1980). *The principle of normalization: A foundation for effective services.* Atlanta: Georgia Advocacy Office.

O'Brien, J. (1987). A guide to personal futures planning. In G. T. Bellamy & B. Wilcox (Eds.), *A comprehensive guide to the activities catalog: An alternative curriculum for youth and adults with severe disabilities.* Baltimore: Brookes.

O'Brien, J., & Lyle, C. (1987). *Framework for accomplishment.* Atlanta: Responsive Systems Associates.

Okano, Y., Eisensmith, R. C., & Guttler, F. (1991). Molecular basis of phenotypic variability in phenylketonuria. *New England Journal of Medicine, 324,* 1232-1238.

O'Neill, J., Brown, M., Gordon, W., Schonhorn, R., & Greer, E. (1981). Activity patterns of mentally retarded adults in institutions and communities: A longitudinal study. *Applied Research in Mental Retardation, 2,* 367-379.

P

Paine, R. S., & Oppe, T. E. (1966). *Neurological examination of children.* Philadelphia: Lippincott.

Parette, H. P., Jr., Hourcade, J. J., & Brimberry, R. K. (1990). The family physician's role with parents of young children with developmental disabilities. *Journal of Family Practice, 13,* 288-296.

Parsons, J. A., May, J. G., & Menolascino, F. J. (1984). The nature and incidence of mental illness in mentally retarded individuals. In F. J. Menolascino & J. A. Stark (Eds.), *Handbook of mental illness in the mentally retarded* (pp. 3-44). New York: Plenum Press.

Pearce, C. K. (1990). Building values into accreditation practices. In V. J. Bradley & H. A. Bersani (Eds.), *Quality assurance for individuals with developmental disabilities: It's everybody's business* (pp. 221-232). Baltimore: Brookes.

Peck, C. A., Donaldson, J., & Pezzoli, M. (1990). Some benefits non-handicapped adolescents perceive for themselves from their social relationships with peers who have severe handicaps. *Journal of the Association for Persons with Severe Handicaps, 15,* 241-249.

Peck, C. A., Killen, C. C., & Baumgart, D. (1989). Increasing implementation of special education instruction in mainstream preschools: Direct and generalized effects of nondirective consultation. *Journal of Applied Behavior Analysis, 22,* 197-210.

Perske, R. (1988). *Circle of friends*. Nashville, TN: Abingdon Press.

Piaget, J. (1952). *The origins of intelligence in children*. New York: Norton.

Pollingue, A. (1987). Adaptive behavior and low incidence handicaps: Use of adaptive behavior instruments for persons with physical handicaps. *Journal of Special Education, 21*, 117-125.

Polloway, E. A. (1985). Identification and placement in mild mental retardation programs: Recommendations for professional practice. *Education and Training of the Mentally Retarded, 20*, 218-221.

Polloway, E. A., Epstein, M. H., Patton, J. R., Cullinan, D., & Luebke, J. (1986). Demographic, social, and behavioral characteristics of students with educable mental retardation. *Education and Training of the Mentally Retarded, 21*, 27-34.

Powell, T. H., Panscofar, E. L., Streers, D. E., Butterworth, J., Itzkowitz, J. S., & Rainforth, B. (1991). *Supported employment: Providing integrated employment opportunities for persons with disabilities*. New York: Longman.

Pueschel, S. M., & Mulick, J. A. (Eds.). (1990). *Prevention of developmental disabilities*. Baltimore: Brookes.

R

Ramey, S. L. (1990, Fall). Intergenerational aspects of mental retardation. *Academy of Mental Retardation Newsletter*.

Reiss, S. (1988). *Reiss Screen*. Chicago: International Diagnostic Systems.

Reiss, S. (in press). Assessment of psychopathology in persons with mental retardation. In J. L. Matson & R. P. Barrett (Eds.), *Psychopathology and mental retardation* (2nd ed.). New York: Grune & Stratton.

Reiss, S., Levitan, G. W., & Szysko, J. (1982). Emotional disturbances and mental retardation: Diagnostic overshadowing. *American Journal of Mental Deficiency, 86*, 567-574.

Reschly, D. J. (1981). Evaluation of the effects of SOMPA measures on the classification of students as mildly mentally retarded. *American Journal of Mental Deficiency, 86*, 16-20.

Reschly, D. J. (1987). *Adaptive behavior*. Tallahassee: Florida Department of Education.

Reschly, D. J. (1990). Adaptive behavior. In A. Thomas & J. Grimes (Eds.), *Best practices in school psychology* (2nd ed., pp. 29-42). Washington, DC: National Association of School Psychologists.

Reschly, D. J. (1991). Mental retardation: Conceptual foundations, definitional criteria, and diagnostic operations. In S. R. Hooper, G. W. Hyrd, & R. E. Mattison (Eds.), *Assessment and diagnosis of child and adolescent psychometric disorders, Vol. II: Developmental disorders*. Hillsdale, NJ: Erlbaum.

Reschly, D. J., & Ward, S. M. (1991). Use of adaptive behavior and overrepresentation of black students in programs for students with mild mental retardation. *American Journal on Mental Retardation, 96,* 257-268.

Reudrich, S., & Menolascino, F. J. (1984). Dual diagnosis of mental retardation and mental illness: An overview. In F. J. Menolascino & J. A. Start, (Eds.), *Handbook of mental illness in the mentally retarded* (pp. 45-82). New York: Plenum Press.

Roberts, R. N., Wasik, B. H., Casto, G., & Ramey, C. T. (1991). Family support in the home: Programs, policy and social change. *American Psychologist, 46,* 131-137.

Rowitz, L. (1984). The need for uniform data reporting in mental retardation. *Mental Retardation, 22,* 1-3.

Rowitz, L. (1986). Multiprofessional perspectives on prevention. *Mental Retardation, 24,* 1-3.

Rubin, I. L. (1987). Health care needs of adults with mental retardation. *Mental Retardation, 25,* 1-6.

Rubin, I. L., & Crocker, A. C. (1989). *Developmental disabilities: Delivery of medical care for children and adults.* Philadelphia: Lea & Febiger.

Ruedrich, S., & Menolascino, F. (1984). Dual diagnosis of mental retardation and mental illness: An overview. In F. J. Menolascino & J. A. Stark (Eds.), *Handbook of mental illness in the mentally retarded.* New York: Plenum Press.

S

Sailor, W., Anderson, J., Halvorsen, A., Doering, D., Filler, J., & Goetz, L. (1989). *The comprehensive local school: Regular education for all students with disabilities.* Baltimore Brookes.

Sameroff, A. (1986). The environmental context of child development. *Journal of Pediatrics, 109,* 192-199.

Sargent, L. R. (1981, Jan.). *Assessment, documentation and programming for adaptive behavior: An Iowa task force report.* Des Moines: State of Iowa, Department of Instruction.

Sattler, J. M. (1988). *Assessment of children's intelligence and special abilities* (3rd ed.). San Diego: Author.

Schalock, R. L. (Ed.). (1990). *Quality of life: Perspectives and issues.* Washington, DC: American Association on Mental Retardation.

Schalock, R. L., & Kiernan, W. E. (1990). *Habilitation planning for adults with developmental disabilities.* New York: Springer-Verlag.

Schalock, R. L., & Koehler, R. S. (1988). *Individual assessment/planning for home and community living skills.* Hastings: Mid-Nebraska Mental Retardation Services.

Scheerenberger, R. (1983). *A history of mental retardation.* Baltimore: Brookes.

Scott, K. G. (1988). Theoretical epidemiology: Environment and life-style. In J. F. Kavanagh (Ed.), *Understanding mental retardation* (pp. 23-33). Baltimore: Brookes.

Seltzer, G. B. (1983). Systems of classification. In J. L. Matson & J. A. Mulick (Eds.), *Handbook of mental retardation* (pp. 143-156). New York: Pergamon Press.

Skrtic, T. (1991). *Behind special education.* Denver: Love.

Smith, G. A. (1990). *Supported living: New directions in services to people with developmental disabilities.* Alexandria: National Association of State Mental Retardation Program Directors.

Smith, J. D. (1985). *Minds made feeble: The myth and legacy of the Kallikaks.* Rockville, MD: Aspen.

Smith, J. D. (1989). *The sterilization of Carrie Buck.* New York: New Horizons.

Smith, J. D., & Polloway, E. A. (1978). The dimension of adaptive behavior in mental retardation research: An analysis of recent practices. *American Journal of Mental Deficiency, 84,* 203-206.

Smull, M. (1990). *Crisis in the community.* Arlington, VA: National Association of State Mental Retardation Directors.

Smull, M. W., & Bellamy, G. T. (1991). Community services for adults with disabilities: Policy challenges in the emerging support paradigm. In L. H. Meyer, C. A. Peck, & L. Brown (Eds.), *Critical issues in the lives of people with severe disabilities.* Baltimore: Brookes.

Snell, M. E. (1991). Schools are for all kids: The importance of integration for students with severe disabilities and their peers. In J. W. Lloyd, N. N. Singh, & A. C. Repp (Eds.), *The Regular Education Initiative: Alternative perspectives on concepts, issues, and models* (pp. 133-148). Sycamore, IL: Sycamore.

Snell, M. E., & Brown, F. (in press). Instructional planning and implementation. In M. E. Snell (Ed.), *Systematic instruction of people with severe disabilities* (4th ed.). Columbus, OH: Macmillan.

Snell, M. E., & Eichner, S. J. (1989). Integration for students with profound disabilities. In F. Brown & D. H. Lehr (Eds.), *Persons with profound disabilities: Issues and practices* (pp. 109-138). Baltimore: Brookes.

Sparrow, S. S., Balla, D. A., & Cicchetti, D. V. (1984). *Vineland Adaptive Behavior Scales.* Circle Pines, MN: American Guidance Service.

Stark, J. A., Menolascino, F. J., Albarelli, M. H., & Gray, V. C. (1988). *Mental retardation and mental health: Classification, diagnosis, treatment, services.* New York: Springer-Verlag.

Strully, J., & Strully, C. (1985). Friendship and our children. *Journal of the Association for Persons with Severe Handicaps, 10,* 224-227.

Sullivan, M. E., & Spitalnik, D. M. (1988). *Case management services for persons with developmental disabilities in New Jersey: A systems analysis.* Piscataway, NJ: UMDNJ-Robert Wood Johnson Medical School, University Affiliated Program.

Szymanski, L. S. (1988). Integrative approach to diagnosis of mental disorders in retarded persons. In J. A. Stark, F. J. Menolascino, M. H. Albarelli, & V. C. Gray (Eds.), *Mental retardation and mental health: Classification, diagnosis, treatment, services* (pp. 403–416). New York: Springer-Verlag.

T

Taylor, S. J. (1988). Caught in the continuum: A critical analysis of the principles of the least restrictive environment. *Journal of the Association for Persons with Severe Handicaps, 13,* 41–53.

Temple University. (1990). *The final report on the 1990 national consumer survey of people with developmental disabilities and their families.* Philadelphia: Temple University Developmental Disabilities Center/UAP, Research and Quality Assurance Group.

Terman, L. M., & Merrill, M. A. (1973). *The Stanford-Binet Intelligence Scale* (3rd rev.). Boston: Houghton Mifflin.

Tests in print. (1989). Austin, TX: Pro-Ed.

Thorndike, E. L. (1920, Jan.). Intelligence and its uses. *Harper's Magazine,* 227–235.

Thorndike, R. L., Hagen, E., & Sattler, J. (1985). *Stanford-Binet Intelligence Scale.* Chicago: Riverside.

Turnbull, A. P. (1988). A life span perspective. *Family Resource Coalition Report,* 7(2), 13.

Turnbull, A. P., Summers, J. A., & Brotherson, J. J. (1984). *Working with families with disabled members: A family systems approach.* Lawrence: University of Kansas, Kansas University Affiliated Facility.

Turnbull, A. P., & Turnbull, H. R. III (1990). *Families, professionals, and exceptionality: A special partnership* (2nd ed.). Columbus, OH: Merrill.

Turnbull, H. R. III. (1977). *Consent handbook.* Washington, DC: American Association on Mental Deficiency.

Turnbull, H. R. III, & Brunk, G. L. (1990). Quality of life and public philosophy. In R. L. Schalock (Ed.), *Quality of life: Perspectives and issues* (pp. 193–210). Washington, DC: American Association on Mental Retardation.

Turnbull, H. R. III, & Wheat, M. J. (1983). Legal responses to classification. In J. L. Matson & J. A. Mulick (Eds.), *Handbook of mental retardation* (pp. 157–169). New York: Pergamon Press.

REFERENCES

U

United States Department of Education. (1988). *Tenth annual report to Congress on the implementation of the Education of the Handicapped Act.* Washington, DC: Author.

V

Vandercook, T., York, J., & Forest, M. (1989). The McGill Action Planning Systems (MAPS): A strategy for building the vision. *The Journal of the Association for Persons with Severe Handicaps, 14,* 205–215.

Villa, R. A., & Thousand, J. S. (1990). Administrative supports to promote inclusive schooling. In W. Stainback & S. Stainback (Eds.), *Support networks for inclusive schooling: Interdependent integrated education* (pp. 201–218). Baltimore Brookes.

Voelker, S. L., Shore, D. L., Brown-More, C., Hill, L. C., Miller, L. T., & Perry, J. (1990). Validity of self-report of adaptive behavior by adults with mental retardation. *Mental Retardation, 28,* 305–309.

W

Wechsler, D. (1967). *Wechsler Preschool and Primary Scale of Intelligence.* San Antionio: Psychological Corp.

Wechsler, D. (1981). *Wechsler Adult Intelligence Scale—Revised.* San Antonio, TX: Psychological Corp.

Wechsler, D. (1991). *Wechsler Intelligence Scale for Children-III.* San Antonio, TX: Psychological Corp.

Wehman, P., Schleien, S., & Kiernan, J.(1980). Age appropriate recreation programs for severely handicapped youth and adults. *Journal of the Association for the Severely Handicapped, 5,* 394–407.

Wolfensberger, W. (1972). *The principle of normalization in human services.* Toronto: National Institute on Mental Retardation.

World Health Organization. (1978). *International classification of diseases* (9th revision). Ann Arbor, MI: Commission on Professional and Hospital Activities.

World Health Organization. (1979). *The international classification of diseases: Clinical modification* (9th revision). Ann Arbor, MI: Commission on Professional and Hospital Activities.

World Health Organization. (in press). *The international classification of diseases* (10th revision). Ann Arbor, MI: Commission on Professional and Hospital Activities.

Y

York, J., & Vandercook, T. (1990). Strategies for achieving an integrated education for middle school students with severe disabilities. *Remedial and Special Education, 11*(5), 6-16.Z

Z

Zigler, E., Balla, D., & Hodapp, R. (1984). On the definition and classification of mental retardation. *American Journal of Mental Deficiency, 89,* 215-230.

Zigler, E., & Hodapp, R. M. (1986). *Understanding mental retardation.* New York: Cambridge University Press.

Ziring, P. R., Kastner, T. A., & Friedman, D. L. (1988). Provision of health care for persons with developmental disabilities living in the community. *Journal of the American Medical Association, 260,* 1439-1444.

Zucker, S. H., & Polloway, E. A. (1987). Issues in assessment and identification in mental retardation. *Education and Training in Mental Retardation, 22,* 69-76.

INDEX